An Author's Guide to Literary Agents

Michael Legat was born in London and educated at Whitgift School, Croydon. He joined the Publicity and Production Departments of The Bodley Head in 1941, and apart from three years service in the Navy, stayed there for nine years. In 1956 he was appointed Editorial Director of Corgi Books, following which he held the same position with Cassell & Company. Since 1978 he has been a full-time author, publisher's consultant and lecturer. He is married and lives in Horsted Keynes.

Contrary to what is stated in the description of the book on the back cover, this book does not contain a list of literary agents.

By the same author

non-fiction

An Author's Guide to Publishing
Writing for Pleasure and Profit
The Nuts and Bolts of Writing
Plotting the Novel
Non-fiction Books: An Author's Guide
Understanding Publishers' Contracts
The Writer's Rights
Dear Author ...
How to Write Historical Novels
The Illustrated Dictionary of Western Literature
Putting on a Play
We Beheld His Glory

novels

Mario's Vineyard
The Silver Fountain
The Shapiro Diamond
The Silk Maker
The Cast Iron Man

An Author's Guide to Literary Agents

Michael Legat

ROBERT HALE · LONDON

First published in Great Britain 1995

ISBN 0 7090 5572 2

Robert Hale Limited
Clerkenwell House
Clerkenwell Green
London EC1R 0HT

2 4 6 8 10 9 7 5 3 1

Set in Ehrhardt by
Derek Doyle & Associates, Mold, Clwyd.
Printed in Great Britain by
St Edmundsbury Press, Bury St Edmunds, Suffolk.
Bound by WBC Book Manufacturers Ltd,
Bridgend, Mid-Glamorgan.

Contents

1 A Brief History of Literary Agency 7
2 How to Get an Agent 17
3 The Agent's Work: Finding a Publisher 43
4 The Agent's Work: Negotiating a Contract 51
5 The Agent's Work: Other Functions 61
6 The Agent's Charges 87
7 The Agent's Contract 95
8 The Published Author's View of Agents 105
9 The Publisher's View of Agents 113

Index 121

I wish to express my grateful thanks to my own agent, John McLaughlin, for the help and advice which he has given me with this book. I should also like to thank all the other agents and the publishers who kindly replied to my questions, and I acknowledge with gratitude the kindness of the Society of Authors in allowing me to quote various details from their 1994 Survey of Literary Agents.

M.L.

1 A Brief History of Literary Agency

In the Beginning

In his book *The Publishing Game* the publisher and author Anthony Blond says that 'agents were originally called into being by the rapacity of publishers'. (He means towards authors.) That may have been a major factor – possibly the most important one – in the rise of literary agencies, but three other reasons for their emergence can be cited: the basic distrust (which sometimes develops into enmity) felt by most authors towards publishers, the lack of business sense and reluctance to do anything about money other than spend it which very many writers manifest to a greater or lesser degree, and, to balance the rapacity of publishers, the greed of authors.

Ever since the invention of printing authors have found themselves in a buyer's market. The buyer was first the printer-cum-bookseller, then later the bookseller who, if he was not also the printer, would employ someone else to manufacture the book, and finally today's buyer is the publisher as the breed has developed in the nineteenth and twentieth centuries. It has been a buyer's market because there have always been more authors trying to get into print than entrepreneurs willing to produce and market their wares, so the printer/bookseller/publisher could (and can) pick and choose. Moreover, since most authors, at least at the start of their careers, do not have the financial means to produce their work in volume form, nor the ability to distribute copies to the book trade, the publisher was able to adopt an attitude which said: 'I have the ability to produce and distribute the book. I put up the money, and I take the risk. Therefore, you the author, should be content with the few pennies I will give you. If your book is a failure – and this is a high risk business – I stand the loss; if it is a success, naturally I reap the rewards.'

Of course, there have always been a few highly successful authors who have become rich from their writings, especially if they could use the subscription system, as Alexander Pope did, to persuade wealthy patrons to order copies of a book in advance of its production. But bestselling authors are always a rule to themselves.

In general, the publisher still has the whip hand today. Self-publishing has become both widespread and respectable, but authors who produce and sell their own books have to be in a position to finance the production and always find that the biggest problem is distribution. The publisher is still necessary for the majority. In most cases, however, although the average author is unlikely to make more than a small amount of money from writing, at least he/she is no longer likely to suffer quite as badly from the publisher's rapacity as in the days before the advent of the literary agent.

Before the first agents emerged, late in the nineteenth century, those authors who were unable or did not want to conduct their own business affairs had to rely on friends. Until 1867, when it was introduced in the United States, the royalty system which is the norm today virtually all over the world was unknown; authors were paid outright sums, sometimes with further moneys payable each time the book was reprinted, or, if they were prepared for a gamble, would work on the 'half-profit' arrangement, which meant no money up front, and a wait either for remuneration, which came only if the book were successful, or for a demand to pay a share of the costs and the loss, which resulted if the book were a failure. Authors as a class are not noted for business and financial acumen, and even those authors who were capable of making suitable agreements with their publishers, whether for an outright or a half-profits sale, were often grateful for any help they could get. Friends could sometimes be found who would negotiate sales, make sure that the authors were not too badly cheated, or even steer them towards a new publisher if a move seemed necessary. Well-known examples of such useful amanuenses were T. Watts Dunton, who worked for Swinburne, G.H. Lewes who not surprisingly represented George Eliot, Walter Scott's publishers, printers and business managers, John and James Ballantyne, and especially John Forster, a lawyer and himself a successful author, who acted for a galaxy of Victorian writers, including Thackeray, Browning, Carlyle, Tennyson, Landor and, in particular, Dickens.

These friends were all unpaid (although one imagines that some rewards in kind must have come their way), and their advice was probably given only on an ad hoc basis as and when it was requested, so that not even Forster can be regarded as a literary agent in the sense that we use the term today.

It is possible, says James Hepburn in his fascinating book *The Author's Empty Purse & the Rise of the Literary Agent*, that the first professional literary agent was a certain Charles Mitchell, who as early as 1851 was advertising his Literary and Advertising Agency, but it seems that he may have been more concerned with finding authors for publishers than the other way round, and the advertising side of his business was almost certainly concerned with acting as a middle man between businesses which wished to advertise and the journals in which the advertisements were placed.

A.P. Watt

Even A.P. Watt, generally recognized as the world's first true literary agent, sometimes worked for publishers as well as for authors, placing various rights on their behalf, and taking a commission on the proceeds. However, his main concern was with authors. There is some doubt about the date when he began to practise as a literary agent – the official line from the firm which bears his name and is still very active today is that his business was founded in 1875, but that he had been working in the field for some time before that. Watt himself said that he started in 1878, but that may have been the year when he felt entitled to describe himself as a professional literary agent, rather than when he actually began to practise.

Just like many agents today, Alexander Watt gained his initial knowledge of the trade as a publisher, working in partnership with his brother-in-law, Alexander Strahan. When the firm began to fail, Watt left to become an advertising agent, and then a literary agent, selling publishing rights, negotiating contracts, and acting as friend and adviser to a number of authors. Before long he had built up, by personal recommendations and by advertising, a considerable clientèle, including Wilkie Collins, Rudyard Kipling and W.B. Yeats. It was he, too, who established the standard commission of 10% which even today is the amount which the majority of agents take from their clients' earnings (although there is a recent tendency to demand 15% or even more).

A.M. Burghes, W.M. Colles and J. Eveleigh Nash

Watt's first rival of note was Alexander Burghes, who is said to have founded his agency in 1879. He had a limited success, but in 1912 he and his son, who was working for him, were prosecuted for a number of business misdemeanours, and when they were found guilty, their business collapsed.

The Society of Authors, which for many years seemed unable to make up its mind whether or not literary agents were A Good Thing, sponsored in 1889 an Authors' Syndicate, which was intended to be a non-profit-making literary agency for its members. In charge of this project was a gentleman called W.M. Colles, whose incompetence and generally poor relationships with his clients made him of little importance.

J. Eveleigh Nash set up as an agent in 1898, but closed his office after a very short time.

J.B. Pinker

Of far more importance than Burghes, Colles or Nash was J.B. Pinker, whose agency, founded in 1896, included among its clients Henry James, Oscar Wilde, H.G. Wells and, most notably, Arnold Bennett and Joseph Conrad. Pinker appears to have been a particularly charismatic character and was extraordinarily interested in new young writers – in contrast with Watt, whose concern was far more with those who were already established. He was also unusual in asking the authors on his books to sign contracts which formally appointed him to act on their behalf, a procedure which has come back into general favour with agencies only in the last decade or so.

Pinker's agency seemed destined for pre-eminence, but he died suddenly in 1922, and although the business was taken over by his son, the latter was later convicted of defrauding certain of his clients, and the agency collapsed a comparatively short time after its founder's death.

Curtis Brown

One other firm which was founded in the early days of the agency business is particularly worthy of note. A young American, Curtis Brown, came to Britain as a journalist in 1898, and was soon acting as a literary agency. By 1905 he had established, under his own name, a very successful firm, which is not only still in existence today, but especially since its merger with John Farquharson in 1989 (to form the Curtis Brown Group) is by far the largest literary agency in Britain.

Early Relationships with Publishers

Not surprisingly, publishers were far from enraptured when A.P. Watt and his competitors began to represent authors and to demand better terms for them. In fact they expressed with cries of heart-rending anguish the pain which they began to experience in their purses. It was obvious, they claimed, that agents would bring ruin upon the whole trade by their onslaught on publishers' profits. What was almost as bad was the fact that agents were usurping the position which publishers had believed they held as the devoted friends of authors.

William Heinemann, the founder of the firm which bears his name, waged a war during the 1890s, which, although it was directed specifically against A.P. Watt, was in fact an attack on the whole agency business. The agent not only comes between the publisher and the author, Heinemann said, destroying the happy relationship which should exist between them, but pretends to protect his clients against the dishonesty of publishers, which is dishonest of the agent, because publishers do not take advantage of authors; agents also not only foster the greed of authors, but demean them by suggesting that they cannot successfully take care of themselves in business matters; moreover, publishers should not be played off against each other, with major authors being put out to auction, especially since any such action does not recognize that an author's success is due in the first place to the original publisher's hard work.

Heinemann quite clearly spoke for most other publishers, and even as late as the 1960s there were many leaders in the publishing industry who were virulently anti-agent. In his classic book *The Truth About Publishing* Sir Stanley Unwin said, with a hint of scorn, that it was doubtful whether more than 10%, or at the most 12%, of published books had been placed by agents.

Not all authors were enthusiastic about agents, either. Bernard Shaw, who was of course an excellent businessman as well as a highly successful playwright, said, 'The literary agency is a favourite resort of persons who have not ability enough either for ordinary business pursuits or for literature.' But then Shaw was always prepared to issue a magisterial condemnation of those he thought to be his inferiors. H.G. Wells, at one time very pro-agent, later changed his mind, and tried to persuade his fellow members of the Society of Authors that they were better off on their own. As has already been mentioned, the Society of Authors itself was ambivalent about agents for many years, especially when, as happened from time to time, an agent was detected in chicanery of some kind.

Agents in the Twentieth Century

The opposition of publishers and of some authors was not the only problem which the early agencies faced. Another difficulty was infighting among the agents themselves, which mostly took the form of blatant attempts to steal each other's clients. (Poaching of this kind is not unknown today, but is usually done so discreetly, with any blame being placed on the capriciousness of the author, that the offended agent is left unhappy but unable to do anything but lick his/her wounds in privacy.) However, despite various teething troubles, the agency business prospered, and among the companies which were set up in the first decades of the twentieth century and which are still active today were Hughes Massie (founded in 1912 and now merged with Aitken, Stone and Wylie), A.M. Heath (founded in 1919, and still independent), and A.D. Peters (founded in 1924, and now part of the Peters Fraser & Dunlop Group). Many agencies come into being when the employees of one firm leave to start their own businesses; John Farquharson, who left Curtis Brown in 1919 to do this, was an early example, and it is interesting that this firm should eventually have returned, as it were, to the fold. But perhaps the most remarkable story of the forming and reforming of agencies began in 1935 when Nancy Pearn, Laurence Pollinger and David Higham left Curtis Brown (which has always been a training-ground and seed-bed for agents), and began their own agency; Nancy Pearn died in 1950, and soon after Laurence Pollinger and David Higham split up, forming their own agencies; Laurence Pollinger brought his sons Gerald and Murray into his business, but in 1969 Murray Pollinger broke away and set up on his own.

Literary agents are now an accepted and respected part of the literary scene. A few publishers may still resent their 'interference' and an over-aggressive agent can still meet some opposition, but in general even those publishers who prefer to sign up their authors direct are willing on occasion to work with agents and to welcome their approaches (see Chapter 9). As for authors, the majority, apart from those writing in the educational and academic fields, few of whom employ agents, are delighted to have an agent and regard them, as we shall see in Chapter 8, as friends as well as essential business colleagues. And of course, authors in general have good cause to be grateful to agents. It was collaboration between the then existing agencies which, in 1919, did away with the notorious 'baker's dozen' clause which had been standard in publisher's contracts, allowing the publisher, when accounting for royalties, to count 13 sales as 12, and to pay on the lesser number. The Minimum Terms Agreement, which the Society of Authors and the Writers' Guild have been promoting since 1980, and which has not only improved the author's financial terms, but has also enhanced his/her status, would probably not have had the same measure of success if its principles had not been approved of by agents, who had been working for the inclusion of many of its provisions in the contracts which they negotiated.

And how the agency business has grown! At the turn of the century there were no more than half a dozen literary agents in Britain; by 1946, *Writers' and Artists' Yearbook* listed 39 agencies; the number had increased in 1975 to over 80, and the 1995 edition has no fewer than 138. For years tutors of creative writing have been telling would-be authors that it is more difficult to find an agent than a publisher, and have based this partly on the fact that publishers have always substantially outnumbered agents. How long that will remain true seems doubtful at the present rate of increase, although whether there is sufficient profitable business to support so many new agencies is a valid question.

The Association of Authors' Agents

Once it had accepted the fact that agents were here to stay and were probably beneficial to authors, the Society of Authors tried to persuade the agencies to form an association, especially of course with the object of producing some kind of acceptable principles of operation to which its members would adhere. It was also argued that it would enable agents to speak with one powerful voice on any appropriate issues, as had happened in the battle over the baker's dozen. Attempts to set up a society for agents were made over the years, and always failed because of the refusal of the major companies to join. However, in 1974 the Association of Authors' Agents was finally established and although it must be said that the largest agent of all, the Curtis Brown Group, is not a member, and certain others have stayed outside, the Association still flourishes.

Members of the AAA are indicated in *Writers' and Artists' Yearbook* and in *The Writer's Handbook* by an asterisk. The absence of an asterisk does not necessarily indicate that the agent concerned has refused to join the Association, or that it is in any way unreliable, but may mean that the firm concerned has not been in business long enough to meet the standards of experience and size which are required to qualify for membership (firms must have been actively engaged in agency work for a minimum of three years, and have an annual commission income of at least £25,000).

The AAA has a 'Code of Practice' which is reproduced in Chapter 7.

2 How to Get an Agent

Do You Need an Agent?

The reason why most would-be authors want to be represented by an agent in the first place is because they hope that the agent will find a publisher for their work. This is undoubtedly the most essential of the functions which the agent performs for his/her clients, and although there are many more services that a good agent offers, very few of them will take place at all if the agent does not succeed in placing the client's book with a publisher. However, it is not only through agents that books get signed up by publishers, and before you start on the task of persuading an agent to take you on, you should first look at the situation carefully to decide just how essential to you an agent is.

The first question to be asked is what sort of literary work you do. If you restrict yourself to occasional short stories, or feature articles, or poetry, you will find it just about impossible to get an agent, because, unless you are a full-time writer with an impressive annual output (and probably an already-established reputation which allows you to write for the major national newspapers and magazines), the income from your writings will be so small that it will not be worth the agent's while to handle your work (and to get a clearer understanding of this point, see Chapter 6). Of course, if are a very successful, established author, your agent will probably willingly handle any little thing that you care to write, simply because he/she loves you (or the commission on your earnings) so much.

You may also encounter a problem in finding representation if your work is designed for the educational or academic markets, since it is quite rare for literary agents to be involved in the marketing of such books, and few of them would boast that they really understand the educational field and its requirements. It may seem surprising that agents have not sought more vigorously to make themselves sufficiently expert to muscle in on this lucrative market. I think there are fairly clear-cut reasons for this. To take educational books first, their authors, working in the field themselves, usually know who the possible publishers are for their books, and since they can often establish direct contact with the comparatively few firms who would be interested, they have less need than authors in other genres for an agent to find a publisher for them; equally, the publishers know that there are plenty of author-candidates for any particular book which they want, and will always prefer one without an agent – educational publishers tend to be extremely conservative in their attitude towards the terms which they offer and are unlikely to look favourably on an agent's intervention, or to agree to any of the concessions for which he/she would ask. That is also true of publishers in the academic field, but the authors of academic books differ from those who write educational material in that they usually produce their work for other purposes than making money (such as contributing to scholarship, or furthering their academic career); publication is necessary for them – indeed, it is of prime importance – but in many cases they would be quite happy to receive no reward at all. An agent asking the publisher for better terms might simply spoil their chances. It is also worth pointing out that there are far fewer opportunities for the sale of subsidiary rights in educational and academic books, so that aspect of an agent's work is not needed.

Again, if you write for stage, film, television and/or radio, you will certainly need an agent, but you should probably look for a specialist rather than the average literary agent (although some of the bigger agencies have departments for such work).

Assuming that your intention is to write books for the general market (or that you have already done so), the next question to ask yourself is just what you want from an agent. The benefits which are described in Chapters 3, 4 and 5 may sound enticing, but not every author wants career advice, nor needs guidance through the intricacies of a contract, and some positively enjoy the occasional bit of conflict with the publisher, while others are numerate and look forward to picking their way through a royalty statement in search of any errors. Those who are particularly private persons may shudder at the idea of an agent's interest and friendship, which they might interpret as potential interference and intrusion into the author's personal life.

Remember, whatever you do want will have to be paid for, and although 10%, or even 15%, may not sound like a great deal, it can mount up. John Hadfield tells the story of J.B. Priestley asking his publisher how much money he would earn from his bestseller, *The Good Companions*, which had recently been published; when he was told that it would be in region of £10,000 (in 1929, when this took place, that was an absolute fortune), Priestley's immediate disgruntled reaction was: 'That means that bugger Peters (his agent) will have made £1,000 out of me.' You may not feel as begrudging as that, but it is worth bearing in mind that the additional earnings that the agent will bring you may be largely swallowed up by his/her commission.

The third question is whether an agent is essential for success if you are writing for the general market, and the answer unequivocally is 'no'. While a very few publishers will consider only books submitted to them by an agent, most publishing houses are quite ready to look at typescripts direct from the author. Such submissions go into what is often known as 'the slushpile'. It sounds a very derogatory term, and suggests that little consideration will be given to the books in it, but although the word is an indication of the fact that publishers expect most of the books which come to them direct from members of the public to be worthless, nevertheless their editors will go through the pile with care, hunting for the one nugget which will turn into a publishable book, and even possibly into a bestseller. Most publishers like to find such books, especially since they have a better chance than with an agented book of controlling all the rights, which means not only that they may make a worthwhile income from their share of sub-licence moneys, but that being able to offer US rights in a number of titles ('title' is often used in publishing jargon as a synonym for 'book') to American publishers may mean that American publishers will offer them British rights in interesting books in return. So you have to do two things: firstly, make every effort to ensure that your typescript is not one of the worthless ones (and that means making sure that you have mastered to a reasonable degree the craft of writing), and secondly, do your market research with care, so that you send the book to the kind of publisher who is likely to be interested in it (and you can do that by looking at published books to see what the various publishers are bringing out, and by asking for advice from booksellers and librarians).

It is worth emphasizing that if you are a novelist trying to get into print, the publisher's slushpile may offer you a much better chance than you will have with an agent. There are two reasons for this: the first is that agents like to take on certainties, or near-certainties, and few first novels, even the well-written ones, come into that category; and the second is that, as explained in Chapter 3, agents will usually give up trying to place a first novel long before you would if you were trying to sell it direct to a publisher yourself.

As I mentioned in Chapter 1, many tutors of Creative Writing will tell you (especially if you are a first novelist) that it is more difficult to get an agent than to find a publisher on your own. At least one agent, David Bolt, is inclined to disagree, largely because of the agent's ability to remain optimistic about a client's chances without having to invest a great deal of money into producing a book, as the publisher has to do. But leaving that argument on one side, two good reasons why it is easier to find a publisher are that there are still a lot more publishers than agents, and that publishers need a constant stream of new titles, whereas an agent may have a limited capacity for taking on new clients (one agent said recently that he has forty clients and won't accept any more because he could not give them a fair share of his time and efforts).

What an Agent Won't Do for You

Before you make up your mind to try to get an agent, you should be quite clear about what an agent can't do for you. The most important thing to remember in this respect is that no agent will be able to sell your work if it is not good enough. Agents won't in fact take on clients unless they believe in their ability and that they have a real chance, sooner or later, of getting published. You must also be prepared for the possibility that, although an agent may accept you as a client, and do so with some enthusiasm, he/she may not be able to interest a publisher in taking your book(s). The publishing business is so often an extremely personal one, in which success or failure depends on personal likes and dislikes, and although an agent, because of his/her expert knowledge of publishers and their wants, may have a good chance of success at marrying you up with the right editor, it just may not work. And you also have to accept the fact that there is a limit to the length of time and amount of effort that the agent may expend on a given book or author (see Chapter 3 for a further discussion of this matter).

The second major point to note is that an agent is unlikely to make you seriously richer. A few cases occur now and then of an agent who successfully hypes a client into the big time – but that never works unless the author concerned can really deliver the goods. If you are among the vast majority of published authors, which is to say that you are not in the bestseller class, an agent will quite possibly get you better terms than you would get on your own, but this will not mean that if a publisher dealing directly with you would offer you, say, a £500 advance against a basic royalty of 10%, the offer would be increased to £5,000 against a 15% royalty if you were represented by an agent. Agents can push publishers a little, but probably not a great deal beyond 10% more than you would be offered if you went to a publisher directly, although you should end up better off, even after paying the agent's commission, and of course you will probably also benefit considerably in other ways, such as better contractual conditions.

A third point to remember is that while an agent may agree to handle only a part of your work – your full-length fiction, perhaps, leaving you free to make your own arrangements, for instance, for short stories or journalism – he/she will not expect to be given only certain of the rights in those works that you do place with the agency. Sò you could not therefore ask an agent to look after the bookclub rights in your book, but not any of the other volume rights. However, an exception to this often applies, as already suggested, to rights in other media, such as films, if the agent is not active in that sphere.

Fourthly, if your work is of a highly specialized nature you cannot expect every agent listed in *Writers' and Artists' Yearbook* or *The Writer's Handbook* to know how to handle it properly. The majority of agents claim to be able to look after authors working in all genres (although some may exclude children's books, for example, or perhaps science fiction) but may find themselves out of their depth in certain fields. Even an agent who claims to be expert in your particular sphere could be exaggerating. You need to check the situation, finding out which other authors writing somewhat similar books the agent has as clients.

An Alternative to an Agent

If you accept that it may be easier to find a publisher than an agent, you may still be worried because, if you go direct to a publisher and get your work accepted, you will be deprived of all the other things that an agent can do for you, and in particular you will not have the benefit of advice about the contract, nor anyone to fight for you if you find yourself in dispute with the publisher. A partial alternative is open once you have received an offer from a commercial publisher to publish your book. At that stage, and before you have actually signed an agreement, you are eligible to join the Society of Authors. The benefits of doing so are substantial, and include free advice about and the vetting of contracts, and action on your behalf if, subsequent to joining, you have a major disagreement with your publisher. The Society does not perform by any means all the functions of an agent – it will not sell rights for you, and it is not in the business of offering editorial or career advice, and although it produces helpful guides on such subjects as income tax, these are necessarily general in scope, and the Society is not able, in most cases, to give individual advice on such matters.

One other possibility if you cannot get an agent is to consult a solicitor (but you do need to have one who specializes in the book business, and they don't come cheap), or a knowledgeable friend (an established author, for instance) if you have one. If you can get no other help, you will forgive my immodesty, I hope, in suggesting that you might buy a copy of my book, *An Author's Guide to Publishing* (published, like this one, by Robert Hale), which gives a great deal of helpful advice on contracts and many other matters.

Neither the Society of Authors, nor the Writers' Guild of Great Britain (which offers its members somewhat similar facilities), nor a solicitor, nor even my book, although they may be of great help, can act as a real substitute for an agent. The point is proved by the fact that, excluding those working in the academic and educational fields, a substantial majority of the members of the Society of Authors also have agents.

Selecting a Suitable Agent

Having decided that you will try to get an agent, what is the next step? This book does not include a list of literary agents, because lists are to be found in those admirable reference books, *Writers' and Artists' Yearbook* and *The Writer's Handbook*. It is worth looking at both, because there are some variations in the details given. Both of them give extensive coverage of UK and US agencies, and *Writers' and Artists' Yearbook* also has sections giving the names and addresses of many agents in overseas countries, including Australia, New Zealand and South Africa.

The choice of agents, especially in Britain and the United States, is large, so how do you know which ones to pick? There are so many imponderables that you might think that you could do worse than choose by sticking a pin in, but in fact there are some questions to ask yourself which may help. For instance, is your book of a specific genre, such as for children, or science fiction, or religious? Some agents specialize, and their interests are set out in the lists, and this includes those who deal with film, television and dramatic rights.

One of the other major questions to be answered is that of the size of the agency. Do you want to go to a large concern, in which a great many agents are employed and within which there will be departments dealing with various aspects of literary work? Curtis Brown, for instance, the largest of the British agencies, has more than a dozen agents on its staff, handling over a thousand authors, and it deals with just about every form of rights that you could think of through a world-wide network of branches. If you were to be taken on by Curtis Brown you would have an enormous range of expertise available, and your work would have an additional cachet because of the agency's prestige. Curtis Brown is not the only large and highly respected firm – it is fairly easy to pick others out from the information given in the reference books. What they have to offer sounds very tempting, but you might find that, as a new author, you would feel a little lost in so large a concern, and you might even suspect (although it is not certain that you would be right in doing so) that you would receive noticeably less attention than the many bestselling authors handled by the agency. Your inclination might therefore be to approach a one-woman business (there are one-man agencies, but women easily outnumber men as agents), where you may not get as comprehensive a service, but in which you are more likely to have a close relationship with the one person who deals with all sides of your work. It is the old problem of whether it is better to be a small fish in a large pond, or a big fish in a small pond, and the answer to it probably depends largely on your own temperament. Although loyalty is a quality which one likes to think a successful author should have, the answer might be to start off with one of the minnows and move to a sturgeon only when you are successful enough to have a great deal of personal clout.

Something else which you might bear in mind is that not all the agents who work for one of the bigger concerns have equal stature. Some of them are comparatively junior, and still learning their trade, and you may not find it easy to place your work in the hands of one of the more senior members of the agency. The really top individual agents, whether they are part of a large concern or work virtually alone, have very considerable power; they are courted by publishers, and they can be certain of selling any books or authors that they take on. But of course, they are looking for the high flyers, and don't agree to represent any old author who comes along. Don't expect to jump straight to the top of the tree.

The lists of agents in either *Writers' and Artists' Yearbook* or *The Writer's Handbook* will give you quite a lot of information in addition to names and addresses – there will probably be some advice on how the agent likes to be approached, and some firms give details of which kinds of books they handle (or don't handle). You will also find that the date when the agency was founded is given, and that membership of the Association of Authors' Agents is indicated by an asterisk. The former information can be particularly useful for a new writer, since it is worth bearing in mind that the newer, smaller agencies will possibly be hungrier for new clients than those which have been established for a long time. The asterisk indicating membership of the AAA is, of course, a guarantee of the standards to which the agency works, but, as has already been explained, the qualifications for joining the Association are such that many perfectly respectable firms are not able to boast of their membership. Other agencies, notably Curtis Brown, have elected for their own reasons not to join the Association although they would obviously qualify to do so. The absence of the asterisk is therefore certainly not to be regarded as a warning to stay away. Further details of the Association, its rules and the qualifications for joining are given in Chapters 1 and 6.

One of the additional considerations which may affect your

choice is the agent's address. I am not referring to the fact that some of the addresses given sound as though they are private houses, meaning that the agent is probably a one-person band and is working from home – there is no reason why such an agent should not be highly effective. No, I wanted to point out that quite a few agents have chosen, for various reasons, not to work in London. Most publishers are based in the capital, and although the majority of agents like to keep in close touch with the editors and to see them regularly, those agents who work in the provinces or in Scotland seem to be able to work as effectively for their clients as if their offices were in London. Anyway, if you live and work away from the Great Wen, it may be worth your while to see whether there is an agent nearer your home who might suit you.

Do make sure, by the way, whether you use *Writers' and Artists' Yearbook* or *The Writer's Handbook*, that you look at an up-to-date edition – it's a changing world, and you don't want to use the wrong address or go to an agent who has gone out of business.

If you have any friends with experience in the world of books (and I am thinking particularly of published authors) it will probably be worth asking for their advice. They may have agents themselves and be prepared to give you an introduction, or they may have heard good or bad reports about various agencies which they can pass on to you (although of course you must accept that gossip of that kind can be very unreliable).

I read recently two conflicting pieces of advice on choosing an agent: one said that it was a good idea to choose one who acted for authors writing in the same genre as your own work; the other said that since agents don't want clones of their successful clients, you should do the opposite and look elsewhere. While it may be true in the case of publishers that they do not want a whole string of very similar books (except of course for a specialist list, such as romantic fiction), I think it applies far less to agents and the first piece of advice might be the better of the two. However, since almost all agents handle almost all kinds of books, choosing on this basis is probably not a matter to lose much sleep over.

Approaching an Agent

Make yourself a list of half a dozen agencies which you intend to try to interest in your work and yourself as an author. You need half a dozen because you may not be accepted by the first ones that you try. As mentioned above, personal likes and dislikes affect many decisions in the book world, and you may have to try a number of times before you hit on the agent who really warms to your ideas. So don't despair if you don't get an immediate acceptance. Most agents have, in their time, turned down clients who have gone on to be extremely successful, so it may simply be that those you try are making a great big mistake in not taking you on. On the other hand, of course, if you are rejected by several agents, perhaps you should ask yourself whether there is anything wrong with your work, and whether it is something that you can put right. It may be some time since you last read what you have written, so try reading it again, aloud; your eyes and your ears may be able to treat the work almost as though it were completely new and fresh, and perhaps you will see some of the things which are wrong.

Reverting to your list of possible agents, you should now compose a letter which will be, in effect, your ambassador (almost all agents like to be approached initially by letter, rather than having a whole typescript or even specimen chapters sent to them). The letter needs to be written with great care. Tell the agent something about yourself, but not too much – you don't need to provide a complete curriculum vitae. It is fairly important to give your sex, age and background, details of your writing experience and something about your plans for the future, and of course you will need to describe the work which you hope to send for the agent's consideration, and to say whether you have already made any attempts to interest a publisher. Let us look at those points one by one.

Your sex, age and background. You may feel that none of these should have any relevance to whether you are a suitable candidate for the agency, and you may be right in these days of political correctness. My main point in suggesting that you should specify your sex is simply that some first names nowadays give little indication of whether you are male or female. As for your age, you will not be surprised to learn that younger writers usually find it easier to get accepted than the elderly, and although there are encouraging exceptions like Mary Wesley, it may be worth while, if you are somewhat ancient, to take a few years off – but don't overdo it. It is also helpful to give your age because, if there is more than one agent in the firm, it could be preferable for your work to be handled by someone in the agency who is perhaps of the same vintage as you – an older author may get on better with a more mature agent than with a young one, and a young writer will almost certainly be more in tune with an agent of roughly similar age. A big age difference does not necessarily present any problem, but may do if it means a totally different attitude to life in general. It is also worth bearing in mind that a young author probably hopes to work with the same agent for a great many years, in which case parity of age may be of importance. As for your background, this can really be quite briefly expressed, and may be worth including only if there is something which you feel is of special note.

Details of your writing experience. In particular, do tell the agent of any success you have had in this direction. Publication is always worth mentioning, provided that whatever work you have had published, whether it is no more than a short article, has appeared in a professional magazine or newspaper (a poem in the church magazine doesn't really qualify), or if it is a book, provided that it has been brought out by a commercial publisher rather than self-published (unless you have had a runaway success, and sold several thousand copies) or published by a vanity house. If you have won a prize in a competition, you could put that in, but only if it was a major national competition rather than something small and local. Don't under any circumstances say that your friends or relations all think it is the best book they have ever read, or less extravagantly simply that they all liked it. Even if such comments are to be believed (and how many of your friends and relations will really tell you the truth about your work?), the agent has no way of knowing whether they are worth listening to as critics. On the other hand, if an established authority in your field or perhaps a well-known celebrity has read the book and is prepared to endorse it, that is certainly something which you should make a point of mentioning.

Your plans for the future. Publishers, are always more interested in authors than in single books, by which I mean that they hope to find writers who will provide them with more than one book, which will often enable them to build the author up, so that each new book sells a little better than its predecessor, and the early books can be reprinted at a later stage, and do better than they did initially – at least, that is the hope, and it is one which the agent will share. So include in your letter brief details about other books you intend or hope to write. Some authors, of course, are one-book people – one book is all they have in them, and one book is all they are going to write. Agents are less likely to want clients of that sort, but it does depend on what the first book is – and you may even find that if it is successful your muse will suggest all kinds of follow-ups which you had not previously dreamed of.

Finally, and most importantly there is the matter of the work which you want to send for the agent to look at. Describe it briefly, including any special details (such as the fact that it requires large quantities of colour illustrations, or perhaps that it is intended as one of a series), give its proposed approximate length, say what sort of reader you have in mind, and especially say why it differs from any competitive books which may already be available. In the case of non-fiction, if you have any idea of the size of the market – how many people are interested in the subject, or perhaps work in the field which it covers, or belong to a socicty devoted to what you are writing about – include that information too; but do be realistic, which probably means reducing your most pessimistic prediction by at least a half.

There is no point at all in failing to tell the potential agent that your book has been turned down by all the publishers in London (if this is literally true there is of course no point in sending it to an agent anyway), or even by a few. It is probably not necessary to reveal any rejections by other agents – the firm with which you are now in contact is unlikely to care greatly about the opinions of their competitors. But they will want to know which publishers have seen the book, and absolute honesty is essential – the relationship between author and agent should never be based on any kind of deception. You may think that to tell your agent of a number of rejections will simply destroy his or her interest in you. Well, perhaps, but it would be a waste of time for everyone if the facts are not discovered until later. Besides, it is possible that the agent would not be in the least discouraged, believing that the lack of interest shown in your work merely resulted from your having sent it to the wrong kind of publisher.

All this information in your letter must be kept quite short. Agents don't ever want to wade through pages of waffle, and that is certainly true at this stage. As well as being brief, you need to keep a balance, if you can, between selling yourself and your work as enticingly as possible and going over the top. You don't want to be modest, but if your claims are too wild they will be counter-productive, and the more factual your description of the book's potential, the better. In short, the letter needs to be both attractive and business-like.

Your last paragraph will seek permission to send your work and will ask whether the agent would like to see the completed book (assuming that you have finished it) or a synopsis and specimen pages. Enclose a stamped addressed envelope for a reply. Be prepared, by the way, for the fact that the answer may come from someone other than the person you wrote to, who was probably the head of the agency. He/she may be too busy to take on new clients, and has therefore handed you on to a colleague. Don't worry if you find yourself dealing with someone who seems to be quite junior – the agency will be overseeing what any inexperienced member of their staff is doing to make sure that your affairs are properly handled.

The Agent's Reaction

If you have a good idea for a book, or books, and have written the right kind of letter, you will stand a good chance of receiving a favourable reply. But you must also be prepared for a negative answer, which may come because the agent simply does not see your idea as a viable proposition. Most agents, like most publishers, will occasionally fail to recognize the potential of an idea, or a book, or its author, and will let a saleable book – possibly even a bestseller – slip through their fingers. It doesn't happen often, but they are human, like the rest of us, and can make the odd mistake. Alternatively, your proposition may have failed to excite the agent because he/she is aware that the subject is currently out of fashion with publishers, having been 'done to death' as it were, or because the agency has as many clients as it thinks it wise to handle, or for any one of a number of other reasons. And don't be surprised if the turn-down comes in the form of a rejection slip, with no explanation of why the agent is refusing to consider you as a client – a rejection slip is widely used throughout the literary world, and is not intended to be discourteous, even if it appears to be so.

So what do you do? You try again. And again. And you go on trying until you have convinced yourself either that all the agents in Britain are as thick as two planks and probably dyslexic too, or that maybe your idea isn't as good as you thought and that you need to work on it a bit more.

The same thing applies, of course, if, having had a favourable reply to your letter and having sent off your completed typescript or synopsis and specimen chapters, the agent then returns it with a refusal. Go on trying (or even give up your efforts to interest an agent, and see if you can succeed by going direct to a publisher).

The Easiest Way to Get an Agent

If you succeed in interesting a publisher in your book as a result of a direct submission, to the extent of receiving an offer of publication, you can at that point, and before you sign an agreement, approach an agent and invite him/her to act for you. The publisher, if asked, will probably be willing to recommend a number of agencies, and you need not fear that such suggestions will steer you in the direction of agents who, from the publisher's point of view, are a soft touch. Very few agents are a soft touch anyway, and though the publisher will probably not give you the name of an agent whom he/she finds particularly difficult to deal with or one where some personal antipathy exists, you can be reasonably certain that you will not be given the kind of advice which will be to your disadvantage.

Whether you follow up the publisher's suggestions or go it alone, you should not have any difficulty in finding a willing agent, because if a publisher's offer already exists that means that you have taken most of the gamble out of the agent's business. You may think that it's a bit rich for the agent to come along at that point, when you have done all the hard work, and expect to get the usual 10% or 15% rake-off on the deal (because of course he/she will insist on taking his/her commission). Well, maybe – but you will be getting the benefit of immediate professional advice about the contract (and the agent may be able to improve many of its terms) and for the future you will have all the other services which a good agent offers.

When an Agent Takes You On

Before you settle down to what you hope will be a happy lifetime partnership, there is one other important thing to be done, and that is to meet the agent for a reasonably lengthy face-to-face discussion. If for some reason you cannot meet the agent, you will have to make do with telephone calls and correspondence, but it really is worth the effort to travel to the agent's office if you possibly can.

The first reason for a meeting is to discover whether you like the agent as a person and think that you could possibly become friends, and whether he/she is someone you can respect, who appears to be honest and direct and firm (without being either overbearing or frightening). It is also important to feel that the agent is both reasonably enthusiastic about your work and at least guardedly optimistic about placing it with a publisher.

You should also make clear what you expect from the agent, and find out what he/she expects to do for you. You might go to the meeting armed with a mental list of questions (perhaps based on some of the headings in Chapters 3, 4 and 5 of this book) about the various aspects of an agent's work. And you will want to know what commissions the agent will take, for instance, on American and foreign sales and on film or television rights, if the agency is handling them, and indeed on any deals which it arranges on your behalf.

Find out as much as you can about the agency too – how big it is, what major authors it has on its books, which publishers it regularly deals with, who its overseas representatives are (and does it ever have direct contact with American or foreign publishers?), and so on. Ask what would happen if you switched from the genre of your present work to something quite different – would the agency still be interested in and capable of handling it; your questions on this point may need to be quite penetrating – you should find out, for instance whether the agent acts for other writers in your proposed new field, knows which publishers are likely to be interested, and genuinely knows what he/she is talking about.

All this may sound like an inquisition. Do your best to avoid making it sound like one – no one likes to be grilled in an aggressive way. Of course you don't want to go into a relationship with your eyes shut, and many of your questions will probably be answered anyway in the course of a general conversation. You should also remember that the meeting is not a one-sided one – the agent will be looking at you too, as we shall see later in this chapter, and will have questions to ask. Since it is a business meeting, both sides should appreciate the other's concerns and should be willing to talk frankly.

You should also take the opportunity at this meeting of indicating the kind of personal relationship that you hope for. You might find it a little difficult to say something like: 'Will you phone me – just for a chat – regularly – say, every other week?' if that is what you want, but the agent will probably pick the point up quickly enough if you can drop a few hints on the lines of: 'I do find it such a lonely business' or 'I always feel so uncertain about whether I'm working on the right lines'.

How Agents Select Their Clients

So far we have been looking at the question of how to get an agent solely from the author's point of view. Any agent is likely to receive a very large number of submissions from potential new clients who are hoping to get into print. How do they choose those authors whom they will take on to their lists? Whether the submission is in the form of a completed typescript, a synopsis and specimen chapters, or is simply an enquiry letter, the first test to be applied is one of appearance. Does the submission look scruffy? Is it illegible? If it is a completed work is it handwritten, or typed in single spacing or on both sides of the paper? If it is a letter of enquiry, does it go on for page after page after page? Ten to one, in any of those cases it will be rejected out of hand. First impressions are terribly important and all the rules of presentation of the typescript, which most of those who go to creative writing classes have heard until they are sick of them, apply just as much to submissions to agents as to those sent to publishers. And, as has already been said, any letter you write should be businesslike and no longer than necessary.

Before the agent begins to consider the content of the submission, there are other tests that have to be passed. Is the material illiterate – ungrammatical, misspelled, lacking in punctuation? Does the accompanying letter make the author sound vain, aggressive, over humble, fanatical, or anything else which would be equally tiresome? Instead of conveying information about the author, does it consist of an interminable series of questions – a sort of exam paper for the agent to complete? If the submission claims to be a completed book, is it of book length?

Then what sort of book is it? Has the author omitted to notice that, as the reference books all point out, the agency deals only with a particular genre (such as children's books) and would therefore not be interested in anything which did not fit into that category, or, equally possibly, while working in a great many genres, does not handle certain specialist categories of books, so that it is a waste of time to send anything of that sort?

If the material has not failed at any of these hurdles, the agent will probably read it, and then make a decision about whether or not it is saleable. We shall consider more fully in a moment how that verdict is reached, but in the meantime it can be said that the book must fulfil its own promise: if it is non-fiction it must cover its subject adequately, while if it is fiction it must be a work which is either of high literary merit or is entertaining (or both), and in either case the prose must be readable and almost certainly needs a quality which can only be described as 'authority' – a sense of the author being in control.

The Agent's Knowledge of the Market

As well as the points already covered, the agent who is looking at a submission from a new client will try to assess its potential and will be thinking about the likelihood of selling it to a publisher, and mentally listing those houses and which might be interested in it, and especially those editors who should be persuaded to read it. This means that the agent needs to have an encyclopaedic knowledge of publishers and their editorial staffs and of current trends in books.

A major part of the agent's business life is therefore concerned with regular meetings with editors, and especially with those who are senior enough to dictate, or at least to understand, the editorial policy of the firm. The more the agent can find out about the sort of books that a particular editor is looking for, and the kind in which he/she is not interested, the less time will be wasted in submitting books to the wrong publisher and the better chance there is of making a sale.

And of course the agent's knowledge must go beyond particular publishers so that he/she is aware of what kind of books are selling throughout the trade, and what are not. Is there a market at the moment for historical novels set in the nineteenth century, or must family sagas have a rather more modern background than that? Is there still a vogue for self-help books (the kind which tell you how to win friends and influence people), or does the market seem to have been saturated? Has the whole world suddenly developed an interest in this subject or that? Will the interest be long-lasting or will it have evaporated by the time the author has written a book about it, a publisher has been found and the book has been produced and put on the market?

As well as knowing what is currently popular, the agent must naturally be able to recognize the kind of book which will always be publishable – the authoritative survey which is likely to become the standard work on the subject, or the book which is so beautifully and powerfully written that it will buck the system and sell even if it is supposedly out of fashion.

This is all very well for the general book, but what about the author who writes on a highly specialized subject? How is the agent going to be able to judge work of that kind? Agents are usually well-read, have a wide general knowledge, and are pretty much aware of what is going on in the world, but naturally they cannot be experts on every subject. Unless you pick an agent who has a personal expertise in your esoteric subject, it is likely that the decision on such a specialist book will be made largely on the basis of what the author has to say about his/her experience of the subject and status within the field in question, plus a careful assessment of the style and the apparent authority with which the book is written. It will be left to the potential publisher to send the book to an expert reader for a report on the accuracy and interest of the typescript.

There is one more ingredient which the agent probably adds in before deciding whether or not to take a client on, and this is hunch. It is rarely possible to measure a book against a set of standard criteria, and this is even more true of authors. Hunch will often play a part – the agent will sense that this book 'feels right', that its author has, however faintly, the smell of success about him/her. Of course, it doesn't always work, and a large number of authors should be grateful for that fact – if they and their books could be accurately assessed in advance, far fewer of them would ever get into print.

What the Agent Expects from the Author

Assuming that the agent is interested in the material and believes that it is saleable, a preliminary meeting will probably be arranged with the author, and, as I have already said, both sides should feel that they are compatible before proceeding to enter into a business relationship. The agent, however, will almost certainly be looking for more than that, and will be hoping that this new client is likely to be earning something like £5,000 a year from writing within a reasonably short period – say three or four years. Clearly, not all new clients meet this criterion, and certainly very few can be guaranteed to fulfil it, but it is always desirable.

It would be foolish of the agent not to seek reassurance about the potential earning capacity of any new client. The commission that the agent will take on an annual writing income of £5,000 is £500 (or £750 if the rate is 15%), out of which he/she will have to pay rent and rates for the office, heating, lighting, telephone, postage, printing, stationery, photocopying, travel and entertainment, and all the other overheads; in addition, unless he/she is a one-person business (in which case the agency is likely to be small, and the income generated by its clients may be quite modest), there may be the expense of at least one secretary, possibly an accountant (even if only part-time) and there may be the salaries of more than one agent in the firm to be paid. Admittedly, the client is joining a stable of writers each of whom is contributing to the agency's income, but for a small or medium-sized firm without any major bestselling author on its list, an author who will earn only peanuts is a liability rather than an asset.

The well-known agent Giles Gordon reckons that on average a client costs an agency between £1,000 and £2,000 a year, and if that is true, there is even more need for the authors on the list to be good earners. In turn, this means that an agent is likely to be most receptive to either an already-established and fairly prolific writer, or a youngish beginner who seems to have talent and who has plans for a number of books.

At this first meeting, the agent will also be trying to assess the personality of the new client. Is he/she one of those who require constant cosseting, with regular phone calls, the permanent presentation of a shoulder to cry on, a listening ear for everything which worries the author whether it has anything to do with writing or is a domestic problem or concern about the state of the world? Is the author going to question everything which the agent does and/or complain daily about the publisher's inadequacies? Will he/she look upon any editorial or career advice which the agent offers as unwarranted and impertinent interference? In other words, will this client be a Difficult Author? A.D. Peters, one of the most successful agents in the middle decades of this century, said that an agent must be a writer manqué. This probably true and is one of the reasons why most agents are sympathetic towards authors in general, and prepared to tolerate quite a lot of angst from certain of their clients, especially if they are money-spinners. However, if you are obviously going to be too Difficult you may find that the agent writes to you after the interview to say that on second thoughts he/she has decided against taking you on. The main point, of course, is not merely to discover whether you can work amicably together, but for the agent to find out what kind of treatment is needed in order to produce the best possible work from you.

If you are a first-time author, the agent will probably take an opportunity during your conversation to explain a few of the facts of publishing life. Even well-established writers tend to have over-optimistic dreams about the likely success of their work, and with most beginners a slightly encouraging letter from an agent will almost certainly have produced visions of Porsches and mansions in the Caribbean and flying everywhere by Concorde. The agent will have to point out the reality – that very few authors make enough to live on, let alone a fortune, and that sales rarely climb above the four-figure level.

One other possibility at this first meeting is that the agent will suggest changes to the existing material. If any publishers complain that agents come between them and the author, they probably have themselves to blame because they no longer offer the same standard of editorial advice as in the past. Any author, other than a genius, needs an outside opinion about his/her work from someone who is knowledgeable and, although sympathetic, rather more detached than, for instance, a spouse or partner. Of course, some editors still take infinite pains with their authors, working with them on their books with great understanding and always constructively. But many publishers have become increasingly unwilling to spend that sort of trouble and time, and over the past twenty or thirty years many agents have taken over the editorial work from them. This has of course exacerbated the problem in some ways – publishers often don't expect to have to do any editorial work on an agented book, and that means that their editors get out of the habit of editing completely. The beginners who hope so fervently to get an agent in order that a publisher may be found for their work may not have in mind the highly competent editorial assistance which most agents can offer, but will discover that it is one of the great benefits that agents provide.

And What Then?

Assuming that both sides are happy with their initial contacts, the author can then go on to sign the agreement which the agent will want to draw up, or the letters which will be exchanged between the two parties setting out the mutual understanding (see Chapter 7).

Once you have happily signed up with an agent you may feel that all your worries are at an end. Don't be too euphoric too soon. Despite an enthusiasm for your work and a belief that it is saleable to a publisher, the agent may not succeed in getting you a publishing contract. The book business, as has already been said, is a very personal one in many ways, and while the agent may adore your work, it may not be easy to find an editor who is equally attracted to it.

Moreover, even if a publisher is found, you may not be happy with the terms the agent has negotiated, though, especially if you are a beginner, it will be wise to accept anything that your agent recommends. Remember, he/she would be only too happy to have better terms if they were available, since the agency's share would be bigger. Besides it would make you happier, and agents like their clients to be happy, if only because it makes for a quieter life.

On the other hand, you may come to the conclusion, despite all the fine words when you were just beginning your relationship, that the agent is not all you hoped. You may have been unlucky in your choice. Perhaps there is a clash of personalities and you do not get on well together. Most agents are fairly extrovert (they need to be), and if they don't keep their brashness under control can be disliked by publishers as well as by some of their authors. Or there could be rather more tangible reasons for your dissatisfaction – you might feel that your agent was lazy or incompetent or dishonest, or all three. Most agents are honest and reasonably or very hard-working, but as in any business there is always the odd one out. You should feel able to rely on avoiding that sort of problem with members of the Association of Authors' Agents, who have to accept its standards and can be expelled if they fail to live up to them, but the Association cannot absolutely guarantee that every one of its members will always behave in the most perfect of ways – they are all human, after all – and in any case, the failings of any of its members may be difficult to police. Moreover, it cannot promise that an agent who is a member will not be either too soft and undemanding in dealing with publishers, or far too aggressive.

If your work fails to sell, the agent will no doubt tell you the bad news sooner or later. Whether he/she wants to continue your relationship, perhaps trying to sell other work of yours, depends entirely on circumstances. On the other hand, if you want to cancel your arrangement with the agent, you are free to do so at any time, even if some of your work has been successfully placed by the agent, although in that case certain rules come into play (see Chapter 7).

If you do find that you are without an agent after all, for whatever reason, you can always try again.

3 The Agent's Work: Finding a Publisher

Editorial Advice

Although the quick answer to the question of what an agent will do for you is that he/she will try to match you up with a publisher's editor who will like your work almost as much as you do and will want to publish you, that is only a small part of the agent's job. As has already been mentioned in the previous chapter, before an agent takes a client on, or at least before trying to sell the client's work, he/she may suggest editorial changes to the book. Many of the better and more successful agents are excellent editors – indeed, many of them began their careers in the book world in publishing houses, and learned their editorial skills there. You need to be lucky, because not all agents are capable of giving worthwhile and constructive criticism – some don't even try to do so – while others have too many writers on their list to be able to give the necessary time to them all. In any case, apart from the few who specialize in certain subjects, such as children's books or science fiction, almost all agents will handle books on a very wide range of subjects, written in an equally broad span of styles, so the specialist knowledge needed in order to make really helpful editorial suggestions may be lacking. However, if you do get taken on by an agent who has a sympathy for and understanding of your work and can offer advice for the improvement of whatever you have written, you should thank your lucky stars, not only because of the immediate value of his/her comments, but because it is possible that you may find the agent of more use to you in this respect than the publisher's editor. Many publisher's editors are excellent – even brilliant – but not all of them have the skills of a Maxwell Perkins (the American editor – a legend in the trade – who worked so effectively with F. Scott Fitzgerald, Ernest Hemingway, Erskine Caldwell, Thomas Wolfe, and many others), and others are overworked, so that they cannot devote the necessary time to each of the books that they handle, while others may be out of sympathy with the work of some of their authors (which doesn't help) or may believe that they are better writers than their authors (which is worse, if it isn't true – and it rarely is).

So, if an agent decides to take you on as a client, you may get a great deal of helpful editorial advice before he/she begins the process of trying to find a publisher for you. Some agents make a speciality of working very closely with their clients, especially in the field of popular fiction, masterminding the structure of the book, moulding the plot and the characterizations, sharpening the actual writing, all to meet current market demands, with the result that the job of selling the books becomes almost a sinecure. Of course, the kind of agent who can act also as an editor will probably do so not only for your first book, but for all the work that you produce.

Finding a Publisher for You

When the agent has taken the author on and the work is sufficiently polished for it to be sent out, he/she will start on trying to interest a publisher in the author and the book, and to get an offer of publication.

The first question to be decided by the agent is which publisher to submit the work to. Obviously, it has to be a house which is likely to be interested in whatever kind of book it is, and the agent's knowledge of the trade is of immense importance here. An author working on his/her own can do a lot of market research to help find a suitable publisher, but cannot hope to have the same information as the agent, who is in touch with the editors, talking to them regularly, and therefore knows not only which are the up-market imprints and which the more popular, and which are the specialists in art or gardening or how-to books about writing, but is also well-enough informed to know that although Publisher A would seem to be just the right house to which to send a family saga set in Birmingham from the turn of the century until the present, in fact that publisher has just taken on an exactly similar book, or perhaps has decided not to publish any more family sagas, at least for the time being, and so it would not be worthwhile submitting the book to that firm. Equally, the agent may know that Publisher B, who would not normally have been thought of as likely to be interested, has decided to enter that particular market and so is currently looking for exactly that sort of book. And the same kind of thing applies, of course, to any kind of book, whether it is fiction or non-fiction. Apart from the various editorial policies which different publishers may be pursuing, editors have likes and dislikes, and some are more ready than others to take a gamble, or are particularly good at nurturing a talent which is not yet fully developed, or are particularly into sex or cars or baroque music – the good agent knows all these idiosyncrasies, and this knowledge is his/her special expertise. It allows the pinpointing of those publishing houses to which a given book is most likely to be sold.

So, just like an author trying to find a publisher or an agent, a list is drawn up. At the top of the list, naturally, will be the publisher which the agent thinks will be the best bet. You might think that the first criterion might be the size, wealth and power of the publisher, and that is certainly true if the agent is expecting to get a large amount of money for the book, and wants a publisher who will spend a great deal on promoting it, and who has a large and effective sales team. You might also imagine that even for less marketable books the agent would go first to a large publisher, because such firms need to find a great many publishable books every year, and so may be more receptive to a new author. But it isn't necessarily so. Sometimes a smaller firm can do just as good a job as a big one – sometimes a better one, simply because the book does not get swamped by all the others on the list, and especially by the blockbuster bestsellers. And smaller publishers want new authors too. It may be much better for the author to be a fairly important name on a small publisher's list, than a hardly noticeable one with one of the giant houses.

One other important consideration is the other authors on a particular publisher's list. The publisher may already have, for example, a major writer of historical biographies, producing first-class books at regular intervals, and will not perhaps be interested in a competitor to that author, however talented and saleable, because of the conflict of interest which could arise (not to mention the possible jealousies of the two authors).

But supposing that there are several possible homes for the work, which one will the agent try first? Agents are normally prepared to deal with any publisher, except those few that they may believe to be either totally incompetent or guilty of sharp practice of some kind, provided that there has not been some awful quarrel (which can occasionally happen). In the last resort, if there is no hope of anything better, a book can even be submitted to a publisher who will pay very little, and not do a great deal for the book – at least it will be a start and get the author into print, and it may be possible to do better with subsequent books. However, assuming that the agent has a choice between a number of possible publishers, all with equal claims to be considered, he/she will undoubtedly put a friend first. This may seem initially a slightly shocking idea – friendship should not enter into business. But of course it does, in all spheres. But it does not mean that a publisher will buy a book simply because of a liking for the agent – it's much too commercial a business for that. A business friendship implies personal liking, but is usually and much more importantly based on the respect which comes from working together successfully over a period of years. Each side knows that the other is honest and highly competent; additionally, the publisher can be sure that the agent will not submit a book which is without merit or unsuited to the publisher's list, and that when it comes to negotiation of a contract and any subsequent dealings, the agent will be tough but fair; and the agent knows that the publisher will make a real effort to produce, publish and sell the book well.

Auctions

Writers who attend classes in creative writing frequently ask the tutors whether it is acceptable to send a typescript to more than one publisher at the same time, and the answer is usually that although this practice used to be totally unacceptable few publishers object nowadays, although most of them do like to know if that is what is happening. It means that it takes far less time to show the book to a number of possible publishers and to get their verdicts, although of course the author has to make several copies of the typescript. On the whole, agents do not submit books to more than one publisher at once, partly because publishers tend to react far more quickly to submissions from agents than to those which come direct from members of the public. Unfair? Well, they know that the agented book must have some merit, because the agent wouldn't be handling it otherwise, and that it is likely to be of interest to them, because, at least if the agent is any good, it wouldn't have been sent to them if it weren't. Moreover, agents are not without power, and it pays a publisher to behave well towards them and that includes giving reasonably rapid decisions.

There is however one circumstance in which an agent will submit a book simultaneously to a number of publishers, and that is when he/she has decided to hold an auction. The book involved is invariably one which is expected to have a major sale, and is therefore going to be of interest to a large number of publishers, all of whom may be expected to want to have it on their list. It may be by an already established writer – a 'break-through' book which will promote him/her into the bestseller class; it may be by a major celebrity; it may be a book which has already enjoyed a huge success in the United States; film rights may already have been sold for an enormous sum; or it may be by a new writer and have nothing to recommend it other than the agent's firm conviction that it will sell in hundreds of thousands throughout the world, and make the author a fortune in subsidiary rights too. Any such books are likely to be 'hyped' (promoted into bestsellerdom – at least, that is the hope, although it doesn't always work), and 'hype' very often begins with the agent. When this kind of book comes along, the agent will send it to all the major houses which are likely to be interested and willing to pay through the nose (possibly with every justification) for the privilege of publishing it.

An accompanying letter will set out the terms of the auction, asking for bids by a certain date, perhaps setting a 'floor' (the minimum sum which the agent will entertain), perhaps making it clear that those firms which are in the running to win the auction will be allowed to make second bids, or perhaps, if the author already has a publisher, giving that firm 'topping rights' (the right to win the auction by offering an amount in excess of the top offer received from elsewhere). Some auctions are comparatively modest, but others deal in the kind of sums which make headlines in the national press and turn most authors green with envy at the luck of the writer concerned. (The vast amounts involved may be justifiable, but can sometimes result in one or all of three outcomes: the publisher may be brought near to ruin by the disastrous overpayment if the book fails; the author may be turned into a monster of greed; and thousands of would-be authors will be convinced that such riches are also within their own grasp. But that's all by the way.)

Not all agents are sold on the idea of auctions, because, although in the first place, if left to his/her own devices, the agent will send the book only to those publishers who could be relied on to do a really good job for the author, other publishers can force their way into the auction, and the highest bidder may not be by any means the best house for the book and the author. Largely for this reason, the bids are not always concerned only with the financial terms, but may have to include a detailed plan for the publication and especially for the promotion of the book and the author. Author and agent may be genuinely swayed by these plans, but one suspects that sometimes they are used to steer the book to the publisher that the agent thinks will not only do a good job of promotion but will also in the end achieve the most in terms of sales and the enhancement of the author's reputation, rather than to the one who has bid the highest sum of money.

There are other reasons why some agents dislike auctions: they can cause bad blood between agents and publishers, not only in the case of the unsuccessful bidders in an auction, but also, if the author is already established and has been regularly published by a particular house, that publisher is not going to be best pleased to find an auction in progress which may take the author away; they require a special skill and attitude which not all agents have; and in any case not all authors, greedy though we may be, really like the idea of being auctioned like a prize bull in the cattle market, and the agents concerned may be aware of this.

Giving Up

Reverting to an ordinary submission rather than an auction, the agent may be very disappointed if the publisher he/she expected to leap at the book turns it down, despite all the friendship. But disappointment must be put on one side, and the agent will naturally try again, working through the other possibilities. How many times will the book be submitted before the agent gives up? It depends partly on what sort of book it is. If it is non-fiction of a very specialist nature, there may be only one or two publishers in Britain who would have any ability to sell it and therefore any interest in it; a more general book would probably be sent to a larger number of firms, but perhaps not more than half a dozen – maybe even only three – unless the agent is enamoured of the book (or its author) and is convinced that, if his/her efforts are continued, success is eventually certain. You may feel that to give up trying after only three attempts is pretty feeble, and that if that is all an agent will do, it is hardly worth having one. Wouldn't it be worth showing the book to a minimum of, say, six publishers? You must remember that, firstly, the agent has a realistic knowledge of the book's chances, and will be pretty certain that if Publishers A, B and C, for instance, all turn the book down, it really doesn't stand much chance of being accepted by anyone else. Of course, he/she may be wrong – perhaps any one of Publishers D, E and F might jump at the chance to publish it – but you must bear in mind the fact that the agent makes no money at all until a book is sold, and that each time a book is sent out it involves expense (stationery, secretarial time, postage and packing, and probably telephone calls as well) which the agent has to stand. The cost of submitting a book to a publisher may make the agent give up rather more easily than an author making direct submissions might do.

The situation is even more discouraging with novels. Fiction, especially if it is a first novel, is notoriously difficult to sell, and an agent, despite his/her initial enthusiasm, will probably give up quite quickly, having tried and failed to persuade perhaps three or four of the larger houses to make an offer for it. However, there are dozens of publishers, large, medium and small, who do take on new novelists, and an author's perseverance is often rewarded. One of the differences between selling non-fiction and fiction is that in the latter case the 'love factor' – an editor's personal liking for the book – is very often a major influence in the publisher's decision to accept the novel. The author who persists in trying to sell a novel directly to a publisher may have to submit it many times before eventually finding the one editor who loves the book, but the struggle will then have proved well worth while.

4 The Agent's Work: Negotiating a Contract

The Publisher's Initial Offer

If the agent succeeds in finding a publisher for your work an initial offer will be made for it, usually expressed in the simple form of an advance of £x against such and such basic home and export royalties, plus a statement of the rights which the publisher expects to have and the territories in which those rights may be exercised. If you were handling the negotiations yourself you might be asking whether the offer is good enough. Could the publisher be persuaded to improve it? Could you do better elsewhere? And if so, how do you handle the first publisher while you are trying to sell the book to the second (and possibly, third, fourth and fifth) publisher? Fortunately you should not meet the same problems in answering questions of this sort if you have an agent.

The agent will almost certainly convey the news of any offer to the author as soon as it is received, and probably with a recommendation for acceptance, or, if he/she is not entirely satisfied with the offer, the news that the publisher is being asked to improve the offer or that the agent is trying other publishers. The improvement that the agent is seeking may be an increase in the advance or better royalties or both, and that depends, quite apart from whether it is reasonable to ask for greater generosity on the publisher's part, on such factors as the author's need of immediate cash, which may mean that a larger advance would be especially welcome, or a belief that the book will have a long life, in which case higher royalties may be of great importance. Alternatively, the requested improvements may be concerned with other matters such as which rights the publisher will be granted, or the split of any moneys earned by subsidiary rights. Some agents will always ask for better terms on principle, but others, especially if they know the publishers well and can trust them to play fair, will do so only in special circumstances or if the offer is manifestly inadequate in some respect.

Although it is usual to give the agent a certain amount of freedom in the negotiations, he/she cannot make the final decisions – an agent is your employee and must always in the end refer matters to you for you to accept or refuse, agree or disagree. The problems that would arise over the publisher's offer if you were on your own still have to be answered, but you should be able to rely on receiving expert advice to help you to make up your mind. For instance, if the agent tells you that an offer is on hand from Publisher X, but that a better deal might be expected from Publisher Y, it is your prerogative to say either, 'OK, let's try Y,' or 'No, I'd like to accept the offer from X,' or even, 'Why don't you try Z?'. The agent may argue and should be able to put forward a convincing case for whatever he/she considers to be the best course, but in the end, it's your decision. (Mind you, an agent whose advice you turn down all the time may decide that since you have so little respect for his/her views, it is hardly worth continuing to work on your behalf.)

One of the major benefits in having an agent becomes evident at this stage when the publisher has made a preliminary offer – at least as far as many authors are concerned. A reluctance to discuss money matters with a publisher is common to huge numbers of authors, partly because they find it embarrassing, but mainly because they are unsure of the parameters within which they are operating. Should they ask for more? What is fair and reasonable? On the whole, publishers don't cheat (it doesn't pay them to do so in the long run), but when dealing directly with an inexperienced author, the most honourable of them may be tempted to offer less than the best terms. The authors don't want to accept too little, but are afraid of asking for too much, in case the publisher not only refuses to meet the demand, but actually decides to withdraw from the deal. The agent knows the ropes and the going rate, and, as we shall see later, understands the publisher's position, is also aware of how far the publisher can probably be pushed, and is unlikely to upset the publisher by any manifestation of apparent greed, since the publisher is well aware that it is precisely the agent's business to get the best possible deal for the client.

The Contract

Once a basic understanding with the publisher is reached, the next stage is the drawing up and signing of a contract or agreement. As already mentioned, the publisher's initial offer will have been fairly skeletal, probably not mentioning much more than the advance, the basic royalties and the territories for which a licence will be granted by you the author. The agreement will now have to spell out all sorts of additional details, and it is at this point that the value of having an agent becomes even more clearly manifest. In past times, a single-page letter would often have sufficed to set out the terms on which the publisher would publish a book – there were few subsidiary rights to add complications, and the publisher controlled everything anyway. Nowadays a publishing agreement is likely to be a long and extremely complex document, and to find your way around it you need to be a real expert. Your agent's checking of the terms and the wording of the contract is a vital part of the service he/she offers.

The majority of agents use their own forms of agreement, but these documents are not necessarily standard, differing not only from agent to agent, but also according to which publisher is concerned, since most of the major publishing houses have worked out with most of the agents a form of contract which is acceptable to both parties. Some publishers insist on using their own forms of agreement rather than those of the agent, but in either case, if the agent has checked the document you can be pretty certain that the terms will be acceptable, that your rights will be protected, and that nothing which is in any way harmful to your interests has been included. However, as with any legal document, it is essential that you should read the contract carefully and make sure that you understand it (which is, believe me, a difficult task for a beginner in the business of authorship), but you should be able to rely on your agent explaining everything satisfactorily so that you can sign without hesitation.

If these standard forms of contract are used you might think that it would be a matter of mere routine for the agent to vet the contents of the agreement. There is a certain amount of truth in that idea. However, every book is different, and the agreed terms even for those which are apparently very similar can vary considerably. Moreover, publishers are not always constant in their contractual requirements, and the circumstances of the author may be in some way unusual. The agent can therefore never take the drawing up of any agreement as a matter of routine, and will need to check everything with care. For instance, the basic royalties may be quite acceptable, but there are all sorts of variations which may come into effect in certain circumstances, such as the royalty to be paid on small reprints or the rates which will apply on sales at special discounts, and the agent will want to see that these are all in accordance with normal trade practice.

The Minimum Terms Agreement

One of the things which has probably made life a little easier for the agent is the advent of the Minimum Terms Agreement, which made its first effective appearance in 1980. Drawn up jointly by the Society of Authors and the Writers' Guild of Great Britain, the MTA is a document which is not signed between an individual author and the publisher of his/her book(s), but between the two authors' unions and a publishing house, guaranteeing not only that authors published by the firm in question will get a fair financial deal (the advance, the royalties, the varying split of moneys from the different subsidiary rights), but that they are treated by the publishers more like partners than they were in the past, with the recognition of their right to be kept informed of what is happening with their books and to be consulted (and listened to seriously) on such matters as the publication date, the blurb, the jacket design, and the sale of subsidiary rights. Many agents had been attempting to incorporate similar terms in their agreements, and some had been successful in doing so, but although the MTA has been signed by relatively few publishing houses and is intended to apply only to members of either the Society of Authors or the Writers' Guild, its principles have become widely accepted, even by non-signatories, and in most cases offered to all authors on their lists. Although some dinosaur publishers think they are still living in the days when authors could be paid a pittance and had little say in anything affecting their books, agents no longer have to fight as vigorously as in the past to get the MTA's provisions, or their equivalent, included in the agreements they negotiate. (For a copy of an MTA and a discussion of its clauses, see *An Author's Guide to Publishing* and *Understanding Publishers' Contracts*, both by Michael Legat and published by Robert Hale.)

If the publisher's agreement is used, the agent will be particularly on the lookout for such controversial matters as wording which gives the publisher the right to refuse to accept a commissioned book without due cause, provision for payment to be made to the author on remaindered copies of the book, and the legal position of the author in the event of the publisher's bankruptcy. There may also be a small tussle over the agent's insistence that the publisher may not assign rights in the book to a third party without the author's consent. In some cases special clauses may be included to cover publicity and promotion plans, or perhaps (if the author is grand enough to demand it) a prohibition on the advertising of any other author's books within the pages of the book which is the subject of the agreement. One thing which will not appear is an old-fashioned option clause, giving the publisher the automatic right to publish the author's next book on the same terms as the present one – publishers nowadays have to earn the right to keep an author on their list, and the terms of the contract for a new book will be negotiable, at least if an agent has any say in the matter. There will also, of course, be a clause stating that all sums payable to the author under the agreement will be sent to the agent. Further details and explanations of the various terms and clauses can be found in *Understanding Publishers' Contracts*.

If there are any points on which the agent and the publisher cannot agree, the agent will consult the author, but, assuming that nothing which is in dispute is of major importance and that the rest of the contract is acceptable, it is usually a case of the agent saying that all arguments on this particular point have failed and that it is therefore probably wise to accept the situation.

The Grant of Rights

If you sell your book directly to a publisher, in most cases the contract will grant the publisher a licence to publish and sell the work throughout the world and will give the publisher all rights, so that he/she can sell or sub-licence US, translation, paperback, bookclub, electronic, film rights, and both first and second serial rights, along with a great many other rights which are usually of less importance than those mentioned. Of course the contract will specify how any moneys resulting from such sales or sub-licensing are to be split between the author and the publisher. If you have an agent, he/she will usually restrict the publisher by granting volume rights only (normally taken to mean the licence to produce, or sub-license others to produce, hardcover and paperback editions of the book, to sell bookclub and second serial rights, and to control a few other minor rights, such as anthology or large print rights), and will retain all other rights on your behalf. In either case, the publisher or the agent will make an effort to sell the rights they control.

But all kinds of circumstances have to be taken into

consideration, and sometimes your agent will allow the publisher a less restricted licence, perhaps because he/she is aware of the publisher's skill in a particular area, or possibly, because of special circumstances such as an existing deal covering paperback rights, one which is more limited. There are also occasions when a publisher will put down a huge amount of money for a book, asking and getting control from the agent of all rights, and hoping to recoup at least most of the initial outlay from the sale of those rights; in such cases the agent may be involved in the deals even if they are finally made with the publisher rather than with the author through the agent. In all these circumstances you will be relying on your agent's expertise, and on his/her industry, because none of the rights sell themselves, any more than the book sold itself to a publisher in the first place.

Although publishers have rights departments which will do their best to sell US and translations rights, the agent is often (but not always) in a better position than the publisher to succeed in doing so, and of course these sales can prove to be of prime importance to the author. The explanation of agents' particular abilities in this direction is that most of them have a special reciprocal arrangement with one or more agents in the States or in foreign language countries, whereby they try to sell the works of each other's clients in their respective countries. As far as the British author is concerned, this means that the agent's colleagues abroad, knowing their own markets more closely than a foreign publisher is likely to do, will stand a better chance of bringing off a deal. In some cases, however, the British agent will make a direct approach to overseas publishers, sometimes travelling to foreign countries themselves, and frequently receiving visits from publishers and agents who come to Britain.

A market beyond that for the volume form can be found for many works, and the agent needs to know where to send material and who to talk to in order to sell first serial rights or film rights or any other rights which he she/may control. Some agents have people within their organization who deal exclusively with such rights, other individual agents pride themselves on being able to handle any kind of sale, and there are those who will pass film, dramatic and television rights to agencies which specialize in such work. But of course the one thing the original agent cannot do, if the work has potential, is simply to sit back and wait – some action must be taken.

In selling any of these rights, the agent will almost certainly go through virtually all the processes which have been described in the placing of a book with a publisher, again using his/her experience of the market so as to go to the most likely sources of offers for these additional rights, and conducting the negotiations. Of course, just as an agent will attempt to sell publishing rights only in those books which seem likely to get into print, so he/she will not try to sell film or serial rights unless there is some point in doing so. It is not worth wasting time in approaching television companies to sell the rights in a book like *An Author's Guide to Literary Agents*, nor do agents bother to send a book which is too British to travel, such as a guide book to Sussex, to their corresponding agencies in the US and other foreign countries (although some agencies have an arrangement with their opposite number whereby each agency submits all the corresponding firm's book to a minimum number of publishers even though the books may be totally unsuitable – a waste of time and money in virtually all such cases).

Whatever success may be achieved, the original agent is always going to be involved, liaising with the author, with whoever has bought the rights or with the sub-agent who sold them, and keeping abreast of what is happening, chasing up any dilatoriness and checking payments and the statements which accompany them.

The agent is also likely to be active, at least to some extent, in the exploitation of those rights control of which has been granted to the publisher. Agents meet the editors of bookclubs and paperback houses, and foreign publishers and people working in other branches of the media, and they talk to them about their clients and their books. This is what you might call the promotion of their authors by the agents, and very valuable it can be.

Electronic Rights

In the last few years electronic rights have been become widely discussed and of considerable importance to authors. The subject is extremely complex and covers a wide variety of electronic uses, and unfortunately few people really understand much about the rights. If you are a member of the Society of Authors or the Writers' Guild of Great Britain you should probably go to them for advice, even if you have an agent. If you are not a member, but do have an agent, then you should make sure that he/she should, if possible, retain control of all electronic rights on your behalf, or at least that if the rights are given to your publisher the terms of your payments are either similar to the royalties that you would get on sales of a hardcover book, or, in the case of a sub-licence, that your share of the proceeds is in the region of at least 80%.

5 The Agent's Work: Other Functions

Keeping the Publisher Up to Scratch

On the whole, publishers are reasonably honest and fairly scrupulous in adhering to the terms of a contract. Nevertheless, largely because publishing is so complex a business (just think of the fact that over 70,000 new books are published in Britain each year – every one of them different), plans get changed, uncontrollable gremlins get into the publishing process, and slip-ups do occur within the publishing house. Since leaving publishing to become a full-time author (a gamekeeper turned poacher), my loyalties have switched very largely towards authors, but occasionally I still feel considerable sympathy for publishers. For instance, I am convinced that most authors expect too much of their publishers. In life as a whole, it is generally accepted that if things can go wrong, they will, but authors tend not to allow any latitude to their publishers. Are they really being unfair? Well, perhaps not, I have to admit, the main problem in many cases being not so much that something has gone wrong, but that the author has not been told about it.

Apart from not telling authors about problems affecting their books, publishers are often poor communicators and are frequently lax, despite good intentions and the provisions of the Minimum Terms Agreement regarding consultation and information, in letting authors know what is happening to their books. Many authors who deal directly with publishers are chary of making constant enquiries about the progress of their books, and especially of appearing to be critical. After all, publishers are in a buyer's market and the last thing the author wants to do is to disturb the delicate balance of his/her relationship with the publisher by doing anything which will label him/her as a Difficult Author.

Whether there are problems or not, this is another situation in which the agent can be of great value, checking with the publisher, monitoring progress, making sure that no heel-dragging is going on.

It also has to be said that the vast majority of books go through without any trouble, but even if everything works like clockwork, it doesn't do any harm for the publisher to be aware of the agent's presence in the background, ready to intervene if need be.

The Agent as Intermediary

Once the contract is signed, the publisher gets on with the lengthy and often peculiar process of publishing. The author may have the right under the contract to approve the blurb, the jacket design and the copy-editing of the book, and to be consulted about all sorts of matters such as the publication date, the print quantity, the plans for publicity and promotion. The more important the author and the more saleable the book the less likely it is that there will be any cause for disagreement on any such matters, because the publisher will pull out all the stops and will be eager to prove the company's ability and to avoid upsetting the author in any way. If, however, you are a lesser writer, you can easily find that all kinds of things of which you disapprove are happening. You may hate the blurb and the jacket design, but the publisher may take no notice of your protests. You may be convinced that the publication date is wrong, that the price of the book is too high, and that the publicity and promotion is distinguished solely by the fact that it does not appear to exist.

And most of all, these days, you are likely to be offended by the copy-editing. Copy-editors used to be invaluable – they not only corrected punctuation and spelling errors and ironed out inconsistencies, but they rephrased awkward or ambiguous passages and checked the facts, and generally made silk purses out of sows' ears (they often got rid of clichés too). And they did all this with understanding of what the author was trying to do and without attempting to destroy his/her arguments or style. Nowadays, more and more complaints are heard from authors about copy-editors who appear to think that they not only know more about the English language than the author, but that they are better writers.

A lone author who protests about any of these matters may not get very far (although there is always the ultimate sanction of refusing to let the publisher go ahead and daring him/her to sue). An author who has an agent is in a much stronger position. Not only does the agent usually have more clout, partly because he/she does not feel so acutely as the author that the publisher, being in a buyer's market, has all the power, but also because he/she is able, despite any friendships, to discuss any problems with the publisher as a matter of business, fighting the author's corner, but doing so dispassionately, without being as emotionally involved as the author would be.

There are also, unfortunately many other reasons for disagreements between an author and the publisher, and some of them can be of a serious nature – for instance, an excessive and unreasonable delay in publication, or, far worse, the publisher's decision not to publish at all and to cancel the contract. In such situations the agent can usually be depended upon to act more firmly and to negotiate a better settlement than the author would be able to do alone.

Even in cases where the agent does not succeed in getting any satisfaction from the publisher at least he/she will not be fobbed off with a lot of bland waffle, nor blinded with science, but will be given some sort of answer which can be passed on to the author. If the author is distressed, for instance, at the total lack of publicity and promotion for the book, the agent will be able to find out from the publisher exactly what is being done, and why nothing more than that is planned, despite the agent's protests (which may not satisfy the author, but at least will be better than no explanation at all).

The agent's role as a buffer between the author and the publisher is invaluable even if there is no disagreement between any of the parties. Very few authors understand much about publishing, which is a more peculiar business than most as a result of the fact that every book is different and demands individual treatment and presents different problems. The agent, as will be obvious from everything which has gone before in this chapter, must have a considerable knowledge of the publishing process and the way the whole thing works. He/she therefore often functions as an interpreter, explaining what the publisher means when saying this or that, and why this is being done or not done, and – very importantly – what is trade practice and generally acceptable, and what is not.

Of course, an agent does not always take up the cudgels with a publisher when an author is upset, but having listened sympathetically to what the author has to say, may tell his/her client to calm down, because there are no real grounds for complaint (authors often get worked up and angry about something which is normal practice within the trade). The author may also need to be mollified if the sales of the book seem disappointing, at least in his/her eyes, and the agent will have sufficient experience of other authors and their books, and of other publishers, to be able to speak authoritatively on this subject. It is useless, of course, for the agent to tell the author to shut up without explaining why, and it is only from a fairly extensive knowledge of the publishing business that the agent can satisfactorily give the necessary information and advice.

A further benefit of having an agent for the author who is in dispute with a publisher is that if the agent feels that the author's complaint is justified, he/she may go into battle (either in the form of a minor skirmish or in out-and-out warfare) on the author's behalf, and while a fairly furious argument is going on between the publisher and the agent, the author is very often able to maintain an entirely amicable relationship with the editors and others on the publishing staff with whom he is in contact.

Of course, it isn't necessary to have a dispute in order to make use of the agent as a buffer. Any kind of communication which the author does not wish to make directly to the publisher can be passed through the agent, and this process has the additional advantage, as already suggested, that the agent can tell the author what is reasonable and what is not. On the other hand, there is a need to be frugal in using this kind of service – if you are forever demanding that your agent should do things which you could easily do for yourself, you may try him or her beyond reason. An agent may be employed by the author, and may even be viewed in some lights as a servant, but a put-upon servant can easily turn into a bad servant. Because of the nature of their business, agents are often more tolerant towards Difficult Authors than publishers are, but they are ultimately free to refuse to represent someone who is a real pain to them.

Finally under this heading, it is worth scotching the belief that agents have destroyed all possibility of the close relationship which used to exist between an author and a publisher in the old days. Agents may seem to be a more stable element in a volatile world, they may be readier to offer editorial advice, they may understand you more clearly, and above all, they are on your side, but it is still possible to establish a genuine friendship with a publisher, who will take a close interest and help to guide you in your individual writings and in your career, and whose whole attitude will be such that you will raise your eyebrows in surprise when you hear other authors talking of publishers as the enemy. If you are lucky enough to have such a relationship with your publisher, your agent, with any sense, will not interfere or make any attempt to drive a wedge between you.

Being on Your Side

You might think that this heading is really no more than an extension of what I have been talking about, but in fact it goes a little farther than that. It is a sad fact, but true, that the majority of authors see publishers as, to a lesser or greater degree, the enemy. They are big (even the small ones are big as far as the author is concerned) and powerful and they have money. They can accept or reject your work in an arbitrary fashion. Despite all the brave words of the Minimum Terms Agreement, in the end they make the vital decisions about how and when your book shall be produced. And, many authors would add, they aren't really interested in you, but only in making money.

I have long felt that this is one of the most potent reasons for established and experienced authors to remain with an agent, despite probably being quite capable of managing the business side of their literary affairs without help. They feel vulnerable without someone else on their side, without someone to fight their corner. Agents are, of course, in the middle, and have to be able to work amicably with publishers, and indeed to please them, if they are to be successful, but in the end their first loyalty must always be to their authors.

Making Sure that You get the Moneys due to You

When you sign a contract with a publisher an advance is usually paid, and, like all other moneys due under the agreement, it is sent to your agent rather than direct to you. There is usually no problem at all, but unfortunately every now and then an author will have trouble with a non-paying publisher, and the agent then springs into action and does his/her best to get the laggard to send the appropriate cheque. It doesn't always work – publishers who are slow payers are very often in serious financial trouble, and this may mean that, quite apart from not getting your advance, your book will not, alas, see the light of day. But if you have an agent, at least you should feel sure that he/she will be tackling the problem vigorously and unremittingly.

The other principle form of payment to authors comes in the shape of royalties, which arrive, usually twice a year at the beginning of each April and October, with the royalty statements. Publishers' royalty statements have for ages been notorious for the difficulty which the lay person has in understanding them, although there has been some improvement in recent years. Even so, the information which they give is often inadequate, and, unfortunately, often inaccurate. It is sometimes hard to make the authors who are victims of the mistakes in royalty statements believe that the publishers are not deliberately trying to cheat them, especially since many would claim (unfairly, I think) that the errors are almost invariably to the publisher's benefit rather than to the author's.

Agents can usually understand the royalty statements in all their various forms – it is after all their business to be able to interpret them – but any agent will tell you that one of the most important and time-consuming of his/her functions is checking the figures in them. Why should it be so necessary and take so long?

There are two main reasons. The first is because of the huge variety in terms for different books – different percentages, different levels at which the percentages change, different splits of subsidiary earnings, etc, etc. As I keep saying, publishing is a very complex business nowadays, and although many general principles apply throughout the trade, when you get down to details, very few of them can be called genuinely standard. Since this is so, the agent always has to get out the original agreement to check the rates which were laid down, to see that they have been adhered to, to make sure that the arithmetic is correct – all of which can take quite a lot of time. Agents need to be numerate, or at least very adept with the pocket calculator.

The second reason, if you will forgive the sort of remark which can be expected from an old curmudgeon, is that it's all to do with these new-fangled inventions like computers – and with the people who work them. In the old days, royalty statements were prepared by hand, and the royalty clerks who laboured over them – writing them in a beautiful copperplate hand – were painstaking, and generally very accurate, because numeracy was part of their stock-in-trade, and complicated sums in pounds, shillings and pence were child's play to them; they were paid a pittance, and of course they were very slow. Nowadays, such sweated labour is no longer acceptable, and there is no need to have any ability with figures, since the calculator, or some other machine will work everything out. The problem is therefore not really to be found in the calculations – if the computer says that so many sales at a royalty of x% of the published price produces such and such a sum expressed in pounds sterling and decimal pence, it is almost certainly right. So why do agents have to check the statements? Because everything other than the sales figures (which the agent has to take at their face value) and the arithmetical calculation could be wrong – the retail price may have been incorrectly shown, the royalty rate may be wrong, the point at which a higher royalty comes into play may have been ignored, and so on. The problem is not simply (as our old curmudgeon would say) that a computer is only as good as the person operating it; modern publishing is extremely complex, and when you remember that one of the ways in which the complexity is demonstrated is that the contractual terms and the circumstances surrounding the sales of the books on a publisher's list are all likely to differ to a considerable extent, it becomes clear that even the painstaking old-fashioned royalty clerk would find life much more difficult in the modern world, even if he was paid a little more liberally.

You may wonder, nevertheless, why it is necessary for the agent to check the accuracy of the statements. It is surely the responsibility of all publishers to get things right in this respect, and indeed is there not an obligation for them to do so? Yes, of course, and some of the royalty clerks working in publishers' offices accept that responsibility and pride themselves on their accuracy. Others, however, are perhaps a little less punctilious, and since it is easy to make mistakes, even in the most meticulously prepared statements because of the aforesaid complexity and the pressure of work which our sophisticated machines do not seem to have made any the less, the agent needs to check. In case you suspect that the mistakes arise largely because those who make out the statements are trying to save their firm's money, I must make it clear that errors occur in both directions – not only in the publisher's favour – are most unlikely to be intentional, and will be put right as soon as they are pointed out.

Passing over the Client's Money

One London agent, Jüri Gabriel, works in a very unusual way, sometimes arranging that the publishers of his authors should pay those authors directly any moneys which are due to them, less Mr Gabriel's commission, which they then send to him, and sometimes asking the publishers to pay the whole sum to the author, relying on the latter to pass over the commission. All other agents, as far as I know, insist that the total earnings should come to them in the first place, promising that they will then pass the money to the author quickly after deducting what is due to them. The Association of Authors' Agents in its Code of Practice says that moneys will be transmitted to clients within twenty-one days of the sum being cleared through the agent's bank account, which could mean a delay of four weeks; in fact almost all agents do much better than that, usually taking less than a week. There may, however, be much longer delays in April and October when almost all publishers send in their royalty statements; since so many of them come in at the same time and, as has just been explained, they all need to be checked, it often takes agents a long time to clear all the royalty accounts. Incidentally, the need to make sure that the statements are accurate is why most agents do not accept Mr Gabriel's methods – how can he be sure, they ask, that their clients get the right money? And in the case of those authors who receive the whole amount due, I suspect that they also wonder how many clients could be relied on to pass over the agent's share promptly and in full. Mr Gabriel would probably say that of course he checks the royalty statements, and that all his clients are trustworthy, but he is pretty certain to remain the exception to the general rule.

Financial Advice and Help

It has already been suggested that agents need to be numerate. It can also be a great asset to them and their clients if they have a considerable knowledge and understanding of Income Tax and

VAT, especially as they affect authors (and this is not only concerned with chargeable expenses, the treatment of prize money, etc, but since an author's income is likely to be erratic, varying from year to year by substantial amounts, there are in fact special tax provisions which can be of considerable benefit to the author). Many authors ask their agents for advice on these matters, and although some will always direct their clients to an accountant, which is sensible (especially if the author is thinking of turning himself/herself into a limited company), but which may cost a great deal, sometimes the questions are ones which the agent can answer adequately without having to seek more expert advice or involve their clients in additional expense. At the very least, since many authors are quite hopeless at financial matters, an agent with such a client can try to persuade him/her of the wisdom of not spending every penny of the royalties which come in, but of putting a proportion aside for the tax man.

Some authors find themselves in real financial difficulties, without enough money to live on, or facing a totally crippling debt. If you are in that situation, your agent may be able to give you useful information about where to apply for grants (from the Regional Arts Associations, the Authors' Foundation and the Royal Literary Fund). You may notice that I have mentioned grants before saying anything about the possibility of getting extra money from your publisher. Publishers are rarely sympathetic towards such requests – and why should they be? They are not running charitable institutions.

Equally, never expect an agent to advance you money out of his/her own pocket. However friendly you may be, and however much your agent seems to you to be like a cross between a fairy godmother and a guardian angel, there's no reason why you should be favoured in that way. Unless, perhaps, because without help you will never be able to complete the book you are working on. It is just possible that if that book is of some importance, and, to be honest about the situation, likely to be a good earner in due course, the agent will advance you a small sum to tide you over. Don't ever expect it, don't ever depend on it, and if you ask for financial help and your agent refuses, don't feel badly done by. If you do get help, your agent is one in a million – and possibly soft in the head, too.

Reversion of Rights

There are normally three main situations in which an author may demand the reversion of rights: failure on the publisher's part to meet the obligations which the publishing agreement imposes; the fact that the book is out of print and the publisher refuses to reprint it; and the bankruptcy of the publishing firm, forcing it into liquidation.

The last of these situations is one in which an agent's expertise is very much needed, because the matter is always extremely complicated. To begin with, there may be a receiver, or an administrator, or an administrative receiver, all of whom have slightly different functions and need to be dealt with by someone like an agent who understands how it all works. The person in charge of the liquidation usually tries to maintain that all the contracts which the failed publishing house had signed are among its assets, while agents will do their best to rescue the rights in their clients' books, often with the hope of selling them to another publisher, or at least of preventing them from falling into the hands of some unsuitable firm which buys up the assets of the failed concern. Agents may also have to fight to ensure that the benefits of any sub-licences which are still in effect should come direct to them, rather than being counted as assets of the bankrupt publisher.

Failure to adhere to all the conditions of the contract does not normally refer to comparatively minor matters – you would not have much of a case if, for instance, the publisher failed to show you the blurb of your book before printing it – but if, without good cause, publication has not taken place, or you have not been paid any of the moneys due to you, or any fault of that magnitude has been committed by the publisher, then you can claim your rights back. However, this is yet another case where the agent's experience and strength can be of great benefit to you, and one of the factors which he/she will take into consideration is the likelihood of selling your book to another publisher if the rights do revert. It may, in some cases, be wiser to stay where you are and hope that the sinning publisher will reform.

Reversion of rights because the book is out of print (which usually means out of print in all editions – hardback, paperback, bookclub – controlled by the publisher) is the easiest to effect. But although some agents may advise you to ask for reversion as a matter of principle, others may again suggest that you should not to attempt to get your rights back, because there is not much point in doing so if you can't re-sell the rights, and there is always the chance that for some reason, good or eccentric, the original publisher will decide, if the rights are still with that house, to give you another whirl. Once again the agent's experience will guide you.

After reversion of rights it is usual for the book(s) to remain in the agent's hands, ready to be placed if possible with another publisher. But even if the book is dead as far as re-publication is concerned, and can be described as permanently out of print, there may be occasional need for the agent's services – to deal with a request for permission to quote from the book, for instance.

Legal Expertise

It is not only in the case of reversions that an agent needs to have a certain amount of legal knowledge. He/she must be well versed in the laws of copyright, contracts, libel and any of the other legal matters which may from time to time affect his clients. And he/she will know what action to take and where to go for advice if a client is involved in a lawsuit or threat of one (it is highly likely, of course, that the agent will have an active part to play in any case, as a material witness).

Acting for the Author's Estate

When an author dies, the agent, if there is one, continues to function in exactly the same way as before, although his/her ministrations may be even more helpful if the legatee of the author's estate has little if any knowledge of publishing matters. The agent will also very often be asked to provide an estimate of the value of the literary properties which the dead author has left behind, for purposes of probate.

Those who inherit from the author need have no fear that the agent will cease to work vigorously for his/her client. Copyright continues for fifty years after death (the period is soon to be increased to seventy years in accordance with European Union directives) and during that period the agency can continue to earn its commission. The estates of bestselling authors provide agents with a great deal of bread-and-butter, and indeed often some jam, and even if your post mortem earnings do not come into that category, every little helps (and if you have been a Difficult Author there is the additional bonus that you are not still there to make trouble for your agent).

Commissions

Agents do not only sell books which their authors have written or propose to write. They also sometimes obtain commissions for their authors. I am not referring to an idea for a book for which you prepare a synopsis and specimen chapters in the hope of getting a commission from a publisher to write the book in question. Your agent can certainly help to place such a book if the idea is a good one. What I am talking about is the kind of commission that an agent can be instrumental in getting off the ground by putting your name forward as a possible author of a book that a publisher wants. It can work like this: at a meeting between the agent and the publisher, the agent asks if there any kinds of books or specific books that the publisher is looking for; the publisher replies that his firm would dearly like to find, for instance, a new writer of a particular genre of fiction, or, say, an astringent but balanced and well-reasoned book on political correctness; the agent runs mentally through his/her list of clients, and perhaps suggests that Ms X and Mr Y would be perfect for those assignments; meetings may be set up, synopses may be prepared, and in due course, with any luck, contracts are signed. It goes without saying that the agent must never put forward a client who would not be capable of doing a good job. Although the publisher will make sure as far as possible before signing an agreement that the author concerned is in fact suitable, he/she will not want to waste time because the agent hopefully but unrealistically recommends a client who could never fulfil the requirements. Agents can only work successfully if they have the respect of publishers, and they earn that respect by being professional, so that their enthusiasm for their clients is always tempered by a level-headed understanding of how the publishing trade as a whole works and the specific interests of individual publishers.

An excellent illustration of this point comes from the days when I was Editorial Director of Corgi Books, the paperback publishers. During one of my meetings with the late Ursula Winant, a very successful literary agent at the time, she asked whether there was any kind of book for which I was particularly looking, and when I said that I wanted some nurse romances, said that she had an author who could, she thought, write some for me. The author was Claire Rayner, who at that point was virtually unknown and who had written nothing beyond a few articles on nursing. I commissioned Claire to write three nurse romances, which, with their successors, were successfully published by Corgi Books, and then encouraged her to move on to straight novels. Even without that start, her high talents as a novelist would undoubtedly have emerged, and she would have achieved the same degree of success as she enjoys today, but Ursula Winant's recognition of her potential and work on her behalf gave her the impetus that she needed.

There is another way in which an agent can obtain a commission for an author: let us suppose that the author is well-known in a certain field, having had several books successfully published by a publisher who specializes in that particular subject; the agent talks to a different publisher who also brings out books on the same topic and asks whether he/she would like the author to write a book, and if so, on what particular aspect of the subject; a contract may ensue. The agent has to be careful, of course, that the original publisher is not upset to find that the author is writing for a competitor, or at least not too upset – most publishers nowadays recognize that a reasonably prolific author may like to spread his/her wares around, and if they make too many difficulties may find themselves accused of depriving the author of his/her livelihood.

Commissions also arrive from time to time without the agent's intervention, when a publisher with an idea for a book approaches the agent or the author direct. This happens particularly with packagers (who dream up ideas for highly illustrated non-fiction books with a large international and popular appeal, and then seek an author to write the text, usually choosing a well-known writer connected with the field which the book covers). Any commission which comes out of the blue is usually to be welcomed, but sometimes the publisher is simply trying to poach the author from a rival house, and the matter will have to be carefully considered by the agent.

The Ongoing Relationship with the Author

Once your first work has been completed and accepted for publication, you probably begin to think about, and possibly work on, the next book. It may have been discussed at the first meeting between you and the agent, or at some subsequent time, and may also have been mentioned in some detail by the agent to the publisher at the time of the sale of the first book, and the publisher may have expressed some degree of enthusiasm. And if it seemed a good idea, and unless those involved have changed their minds, there is no problem and you will be able to go ahead quite happily. An alternative scenario is that, although a second book was not discussed when the first one was signed up, the publisher has since then talked to you about a follow-up book, and may even have commissioned it.

Both these situations are probably very pleasant for you, but in either case you should not forget the advisability of talking things over with the agent. Quite apart from keeping him/her informed, the agent may have an input to make, and in any case will give you that encouragement which any writer needs.

On the other hand, you may not be at all sure what to write next, and the publisher may be uncertain of how the first book will go and may be waiting to see what happens before making any mention of a second book, let alone a commitment of some kind. The agent, eager to make sure that the client is going to produce more work and that it is going to be on the right lines, has to make a decision about the next course of action. Should the author be left alone to work out what the next book will be, or should the agent try to force the issue, perhaps by suggesting various ideas? The answer to these questions depends, of course, on what sort of person the author is. Agents need to be psychologists, and to recognize the varying natures and needs of their clients. Some authors do not want any help of this kind (they are often solitaries, who speak to their publishers and agents as rarely as possible, preferring to shut themselves away and get on with the job of writing). Others may not merely welcome discussion and ideas, but actually depend totally on an outside stimulus to find out what they will write next.

Whatever the outcome of your discussions with the publisher and the agent, the latter will naturally be involved with any contract which is eventually made, and will undertake all the other functions already described, including the giving of editorial advice.

One of the issues which may come up as early as the second book, but more likely at a later stage, is whether the author should remain with the same publisher. Publishers complained regularly in the early days of agenting that agents moved their authors around from house to house far too often, merely for the sake of a slightly larger advance each time, thus destroying the publisher's efforts to build up an author, not to mention making it impossible for any worthwhile relationship to develop between author and publisher. The modern agent is perhaps more ready to recognize the value of loyalty to the publisher who launched the author, and will certainly be reluctant for the sake of a comparatively small amount of extra money to leave one reasonably competent house and go to another which will do much the same sort of job. However, there are still occasions when it makes good sense to move. Sometimes it is because the author and the publisher have turned out to be incompatible, and sometimes because the publisher has failed badly to publish the book satisfactorily, in either of which cases the initiative may have come as readily from the author as from the agent. Alternatively, a change may be on the cards because the agent believes that another imprint would do substantially better, and sometimes (and this is when the yells of anguish are likely to be at their loudest) when the move does involve an enormously higher advance than the author has ever received before – a change of publisher of this kind may be the only way in which the agent can propel the client into the big time, because the original publisher has got stuck in a rut with the author and can't get out of it.

Whatever the reason for the move, the agent must always consider the fact that the books published by the author's present publisher, and the rights in them granted to that firm, will have to stay there, at least until they go out of print and a reversion order can be lodged. This may not be helpful to the author, because once the move has taken place the original publisher will have far less reason than before to try to promote the author and sell his/her books.

Of course, any move must have the approval of the author, and, despite the agent's arguments and advice, this may not be given all that swiftly by an author who finds his publisher to be particularly sympathetic. This sort of situation highlights the strange relationship that can exist: the author hires the agent and pays for the management of his/her literary affairs, but remains the final arbiter – the author is the employer, and the agent the employee – and can reject the agent's advice, and indeed can sack the agency at any time he/she wishes.

A different set of circumstances applies if the move from one publisher to another is not engineered by either the author or the agent, but occurs because the publisher is taken over by another concern. This can be a very difficult experience for the author, who is quite likely to lose the editor with whom he/she has been working, who is very much in tune with the book, and to find himself landed on the desk of another editor who already has more work than he/she can handle and who hasn't the least interest in the author or the book. In a situation like this, the agent can be very helpful, bringing pressure to bear in order perhaps to move the author to a different editor who will be more sympathetic.

Incidentally, if the idea of staying loyal to one publisher over a long period of time has lost the force it once had, there are two main reasons for the change (apart from the fact that some of the virtues like loyalty are less in fashion nowadays than they used to be): the first is the frequency with which ownership of publishing firms changes hands and the increasing likelihood of an author having to work with a whole string of different editors as one after another they are made redundant or leave of their own volition; and the second is the disappearance of the option clause, which meant that apparent loyalty was no more than a contractual obligation which authors were not strong enough to fight.

Career Advice

An agent can not only give you encouragement, if appropriate, about your proposed second and subsequent books, or discouragement if it seems that you are producing something which the agent knows from experience to be unlikely to appeal, or if you are moving into a whole area in which it would be difficult to sell your work, but may be able to help you to plan your writing work for some years ahead. In certain cases an agent may be able to negotiate a contract covering a number of books to be written over a substantial period of time, and this will give you confidence and a certain financial security, and (if you are the kind of writer who wants this) a good motive for keeping your nose to the grindstone.

One of the functions of a publisher's editor is to dream up ideas for new books, but when they do so do not necessarily have a particular author in mind. Agents can do the same sort of thing, but in their case will usually be aiming the idea specifically at one of their clients. Not all authors require this kind of service from their agents, but most agents will offer it to those of their clients who want it, and some of them are very good at putting ideas forward in this way. Sometimes it is a matter of suggesting what your next book should be in your normal genre, but an imaginative and sensitive agent may detect a potential in your work for you to write something quite different from anything that you had originally intended, and if the perception is correct and if you accept the suggestion, the agent may, by steering you from one kind of writing to another, also steer you from comparative lack of success to fame and fortune.

In short, another of the great advantages of having an agent is that it is part of his/her function to offer not only advice about the second book, but indeed about your entire writing career. And the guidance doesn't stop there, because (although, as has been previously said, you should not bother your agent unnecessarily) an agent usually has a mine of useful information available for his/her clients about all sorts of other things: how to apply for Public Lending Right (in which, incidentally, neither publishers nor agents have a share – nor should either be asked to apply on your behalf), how to get a ticket for the British Museum Reading Room, what constitutes 'fair dealing' (the system which allows you in certain circumstances to quote a limited amount of copyright material without seeking permission), etc, etc.

Promotion of the Author

This heading does not refer to the kind of promotion and publicity that a publisher gives (or often does not give) to a book or an author, but to what the agent can do to build up the author's standing within the book world. An author's status is immediately increased to some extent by the mere fact of having an agent, because any publisher knows that an agent would not be handling that client's work unless he/she believed it to be not only saleable, but capable of generating a sufficient income to make the agent's share worthwhile. But it goes beyond that, and an agent can promote an author by selling his/her work to foreign publishers or other media, by persuading potential sub-licensees to enquire about those subsidiary rights which the publisher controls, by ensuring that the publisher enters the author's work for any appropriate prizes and takes any other opportunity which may present itself for the enhancing of the author's reputation, and in general by talking about the client to all and sundry in a way which excites interest in him/her.

Encouragement

I mentioned briefly, in the context of career advice, the agent's ability to help his/her clients by giving encouragement, and a little more should be said about this aspect, because it is relevant not only in the long term business of building up an author's whole approach to and planning of his or her work, but also in the short term on a day-to-day basis. Authors are often subject to volatile moods, and one day's euphoria (perhaps when a publisher has signed a contract) can be succeeded by quite severe depression, especially since one of the common manifestations of an author's general insecurity is a lack of confidence in whatever he or she is writing at the time. The agent's words of encouragement can be of enormous help, and since an understanding of the author's psychology is a necessity for an agent, most of them are prepared to spend a lot of their time boosting the author's fragile ego and are expert at choosing the right words to do so.

Stability in a Volatile World

The publishing scene is one of constant change these days. Firms are taken over, firms merge, firms go bankrupt, firms stay much as they were but trade under a new name. And publishing personnel flit about from one job to another like a swarm of flies in summertime. You establish a relationship with a publisher – perhaps with a particular editor – and everything is fine, until you turn around to find that the publisher has sold out, and the editor has joined another company, and the real problem is that no one in the new set-up is interested in you or your book, and you can't even follow the editor to his/her new job, partly because of all the contractual problems which such a move would present, but chiefly because the editor's new firm doesn't ever publish your kind of book. Even if the changes are less traumatic for you than that scenario, anything which rocks the author's little boat, undermining confidence and a feeling of security, can be very disturbing. In this volatile world, the agent usually provides an island of stability where the beleaguered author can find refuge. Of course, agents move around too, from time to time, or retire, or get swallowed up by bigger agencies, but not with anything like the same frequency as publishers and their personnel.

Availability

Any author who has ever tried telephoning his/her editor (or anyone in the publishing house other than the telephonist or the latest junior recruit to the accounts department) will be quite used to being told that he/she is 'in a meeting'. All publishers spend most of their time 'in a meeting' – that is a law of nature, and there's nothing to be done about it. This may be – well, of course, it is – an exaggeration, but publishing people are very often difficult to get hold of, and for a variety of reasons in addition to being 'in a meeting'. Editors have to go out to meet people, including authors, they have to travel to visit foreign publishers, they have to attend book fairs, they have sometimes to go to their homes or some other retreat in order to work on a book without constant interruptions in the office, they have to have holidays now and then (and it is neither polite nor kind to ask, 'Why?'), and an awful lot of meetings do in fact take place in most publishers' offices, and are essential in order to keep things running with reasonable smoothness. As I seem to keep saying, publishing is a complex business, and although in the old days it was pretty leisurely and gentlemanly, it is so no longer. Publishers still have long business lunches, but not nearly so often as they used to, and the scurrying about that is forced upon them is likely to be watched by time-and-motion people, or at the very least by a cost-conscious accountant, who will soon put a stop to time- and money-wasting activities, such as the unproductive business of chatting to authors.

So, if you can't talk to your publisher, who can you talk to? Right – your agent. Agents are busy people too, and they have to do many of the same things as editors, such as showing up at book fairs, and entertaining clients, and somehow finding time to read (and give useful advice on) the latest effort by one of the authors on their list. But on the whole, agents, while working no less hard (well, I hope that's true), are able to concentrate their efforts rather more easily on the comparatively small number of clients that each of them handles. And their task is made easier by the fact that, although every client list will include some authors who need constant attention, many of their writers will happily remain dormant, as it were, while writing their books, surfacing only when a new typescript is completed or a new project needs to be got off the ground. All of which adds up to the fact that an agent can often be more readily available than a publisher, and it is something which authors greatly appreciate. Writing, as authors will always tell you with a kind of pride, is a lonely business, and it is good to have someone there, easily accessible, with whom to discuss writing problems, or whom one can telephone just a for a chat.

Friendship

The relationship between an author and an agent is essentially a business one – the two would never come together if it weren't for a wish to gain from each other's abilities, and indeed, whereas the author, unless very successful, can hope to make little more than pin money, and may be far more interested in getting into print than in the financial rewards, the agent depends on his/her authors to make a living, and would not have taken them on as clients in the first place without some belief in their ability to write saleable books. The publishing business, of which agents are a part, has become increasingly hard-headed over the last few decades. No longer 'an occupation for gentlemen', it is profit-driven, tough and ruthless – the kind of world in which there is no room for sentimentality or sympathy for personal feelings, and in which a lot of 'friendships' are based solely on the financial rewards they generate and last only as long as they continue to be profitable for both parties.

Many publishers, especially editors, would deny the truth of that last statement, claiming that their friendships with their authors are genuine and long-lasting. In some cases, perhaps. But you might be surprised, dear reader, to know that, underneath the amiability of many author-publisher friendships often lurks a considerable antipathy.

It all sounds very unpleasant, but happily there is better news in respect of authors and agents. Their relationship may indeed be a business one, but this does not necessarily, or even usually, preclude the possibility of a real friendship developing. Of course, agents vary enormously in personality, just as authors do, and in some cases certain of their authors may find them unsympathetic to a greater or lesser extent. They tend to be outgoing people, and the demands of their work mean that very often they are forceful and possibly even abrasive. But they are also almost always warm at heart, and frequently more tolerant of the quirks of their authors than the latter may be of those of their agents. Some authors shy away from the slightest personal involvement with the agent, and want no more than formal business dealings with them. Most authors find, however, that one of the greatest benefits of having an agent is that he/she becomes a genuine friend. That can be worth a tremendous amount.

Looking for Clients

It may surprise some readers to learn that, despite the facts that it is very hard to get an agent and that agents receive hundreds, if not thousands, of submissions every year, agents actually spend a part of their time actively looking for new clients. Just like publishers, they sometimes approach celebrities who have not yet written a book, and might do so and suggest that representation would help to secure a good deal; they ferret around to find out whether this already published author has an agent, and if not, whether he/she might be persuaded to join the agent's stable; of course, they wouldn't dream of stealing each other's clients – at least, that is what they would tell you – but it is far from unheard-of for an agent to suggest to a major author that if ever that author wished to make a change, a welcome would be waiting.

Keeping in Touch

Agents constantly keep their eyes and ears open. They read newspapers and books and (avidly) the trade press, in order to keep abreast of trends and in particular so that they know what is going on in the book business, which publishers are doing well and which badly, what kinds of books are selling best, what the going rates are for advances and royalties, what new developments are taking place. They almost invariably accept any invitations which come their way to attend trade parties, and they go to trade fairs, including the major annual trade fair in Frankfurt. Trade gossip is not just fun – it's an essential source of vital information.

Above all, literary agents keep in touch with their authors and with publishers. Their authors are of course their life blood, and they need to be cherished, fussed over or not fussed over, as the case may be, but always encouraged and helped and advised, and telephoned and written to and entertained. They must also be promoted whenever the agent has the opportunity of doing anything which will boost their reputations and their sales.

Publishers, on the other hand, are the agents' prime customers, and regular meetings with them must take place, often over lunch, which allows time for friendship and understanding to grow as well as for business to be done. (In fact, the initiative in arranging meetings is more often taken by the publishers, most of whom try constantly to ingratiate themselves with agents.) With both authors and publishers, agents have to try always to maintain friendly relations, avoiding subjects which will provoke arguments of a personal nature, being tough when necessary, but keeping both clients and customers happy.

The Size of the Business

An agent's life is a busy one, as can be gathered from all that has gone before in this chapter. It is also stimulating and has the great advantage of being varied, so that it never if ever becomes boring. But its pressures mean that an agent can effectively handle only a limited number of clients. There seems to be a fairly general agreement in the trade that the optimum number is forty. But of course authors are not all prolific, do not all demand constant attention, and their books and contracts and royalty statements may all go through without needing much attention from the agent.

So the ideal is perhaps forty averagely active authors. That number will allow the agent to operate reasonably effectively, and may also allow him/her a little time for thinking, and since it is a creative business, thinking-time is needed. And of course, the agent, like anyone else, needs a certain amount of leisure in which to pursue whatever his/her interests may be, from writing novels to hunting to playing the recorder (they are not all writers manqué).

Summing Up

Literary agents, like most people, can be divided into three groups – the good, the bad, and those in the middle who are neither markedly good nor distinctly bad. Bad agents will do very few of the things listed in this chapter and only some of those covered in Chapters 3 and 4; the large numbers of agents in the middle category will work rather more satisfactorily; but it is only the good ones who will prove themselves to be a great deal more than mere placers of books and negotiators of contracts (and even they, being human, may not achieve perfection for all of their clients for all of the time).

In his study of publishing *The Book Book*, Anthony Blond neatly sums up the work of the agent: 'The author-publisher relationship has been likened to marriage and, like that delicate institution, it needs a broker to bring the couple together in the first place, someone to arrange the contract and to bless the union, someone, too, who will arbitrate when quarrels occur, be a guidance counsellor when life gets rough and a midwife when birth is imminent. The literary agent is marriage broker, mediator and midwife, negotiator, arbitrator and friend.' But one could with justification add: 'And a great deal more – provided, of course, that one is talking of a good agent.'

6 The Agent's Charges

Pay As You Earn

It is very difficult in this materialistic world to find any service which is genuinely free, unless perhaps it is funded by the Government (and of course we all pay for that). Agents certainly do not receive any State aid, but nevertheless provide a service for which there is no charge until they are successful. They may devote a lot of time to an author and his/her book, and they may spend quite a bit of money in postage and telephone calls when submitting the book to a number of publishers, but if they don't make a sale, there is no charge to the author. Most agents don't even demand a reading fee for looking at all the hundreds of typescripts which land on their desks every year; indeed, members of the Association of Authors' Agents are bound not to charge a reading fee (although it has to be said that not all members adhere strictly to this rule, and the practice of charging for reading, which is increasingly common in the United States, may one day become commonplace in the UK too). You may find, if the agent submits an analytical report on your work, consisting of considerably more than a mere sentence or two, that it will cost you a modest sum, but this will usually apply only if the agent is not intending to handle the work, and you will probably be quite willing to pay a few pounds for the helpful advice which the report gives. Apart from that, no charge is normally made until your work has been sold and money in the form of an advance, royalties or a fee has been received. This means of course that agents do all their initial work on spec – if they fail, despite much effort, to achieve a sale, they get nothing. This may help to explain why beginners often find it difficult to get an agent – you are not likely to be taken on unless the agent feels that there is a really good chance of selling your work.

Commission Rates

When A.P. Watt set up the first literary agency it appears that his decision to charge his clients 10% of their earnings was a fairly arbitrary one. He based it on what advertising agents charged at that period, which seemed a reasonable reward for him and one to which his authors would not object, especially since he hoped to increase their writing income even after his cut. Where British agents and authors were concerned, the basic 10% remained until comparatively recently the standard rake-off on all earnings originating in Britain (that is to say, on payments by British publishers and other licensees to the author whether the sales of their products were made in this country or in overseas markets). Now, however, a few agents charge 12½%, quite a number take 15%, and one or two go even higher and extract 17½% or 20%. The recent survey conducted by the Society of Authors even produced a report on one agent who charged 25%.

Rates on earnings from publication in foreign countries (i.e. usually from US or translation rights) can be expected to come in at 20%, because two agents are involved – the British agent's corresponding agent (sometimes called a sub-agent) in the foreign country takes his/her 10% of the foreign earnings before passing the balance to the British agent, who lops off another 10%. A little elementary arithmetic will demonstrate that the total commission under that arrangement should be 19% rather than 20%, which is true, but many agents round the figure up to their own advantage. Of course, if either agent is in the habit of taking more than 10% the total cut is likely to increase. On the other hand, some agents do their own selling abroad, and may then take only their basic amounts (i.e. 10% or 15% in most cases). It is all rather confusing, and needs to be carefully sorted out when you first sign up with an agent.

Commission rates on articles, short stories and serials sold to magazines and newspapers, and on film, television and stage rights vary from agent to agent, and are often fixed on an ad hoc basis only when the circumstances arise. However, they are very rarely less than 15%. Very occasionally a situation will occur in which an agent will not take any fee at all. It all depends on your basic arrangement with the agent. As an illustration of what I mean, my own agent was instrumental recently in getting me a reasonably well-paid commission to write an article for a specialist publication; he does not normally handle any journalism that I do, and did not charge me commission on this piece of work, although he would have been entitled to do so. You might say, of course, that he didn't have to do any work after the initial introduction, such as negotiating the fee and checking the contract letter and collecting the money and passing it to me, but that would not have been particularly arduous, and I reckon that his commission on the deal would still have left him in pocket. So it was generous, but not, I think, untypical of a good agent.

VAT

All agents have to charge VAT on the payments they make to authors. That does not matter if you earn enough from your writings to be registered for VAT, because you can claim back the tax. But how many authors receive sufficient to register? Of course, you can apply for registration even if your earnings would not really justify it, but the chore of VAT returns hardly makes this worth considering. The fact is, then, that for the majority of writers the moneys received from the agent have had, according to the current rate of VAT, 11.75% deducted if the agent's cut is 10%, 17.625% if it is 15%, and 23.5% if it is 20%. It makes a difference.

Although I have felt it necessary to point out this apparently hidden extra cost, I must also in fairness say that almost all authors who have an agent feel that the VAT is simply a necessary evil which has to be accepted, as it has on most of our purchases and expenses, and that it does not substantially alter the benefit of having an agent.

What is a Fair Rate?

Is it fair for an agent to take more than 10% on your earnings from a book published in the British market? You might wonder whether those agents who charge higher rates of commission give any better service than those who stick to 10%. Almost certainly they do not, but it is not really a matter of fairness or of degrees in the quality of service. Overheads, postage (especially foreign postage), travel, entertainment – the costs have all shot up, and the problem is particularly acute for the small agent, who may also find, as one such explained recently, that an additional financial burden had been placed on her by the amount of form-filling now required in respect of various taxes, insurance, etc, which, because it is yet another acutely time-consuming chore, has forced her to employ a book-keeper to do work which previously she could manage herself.

You might expect that the increases in the agent's costs, which are principally due to inflation, would be covered by parallel increases in the advances and royalties which authors receive. But although some of the really big names can ask for larger and larger sums, in most cases advances and earnings have gone down in recent years, rather than up.

The plain fact is that it will not be all that many years before all agents will have increased their charges. For a start, many will follow the example of those who have already adopted a compromise position, charging 15% on British earnings on the author's first book (which is the one which demands the most work from the agent), but reverting to 10% for subsequent books. And, because their costs continue to rise in line with inflation, and, with the exception of those of the bestsellers, authors' earnings continue to decline, it probably won't be all that long before 15% has become the normal basic fee (with the bolder agencies taking 17½%) and 20% will be charged on first books.

What will happen when the cost of having an agent rises dramatically? Some authors will perhaps decide that they can manage perfectly well on their own, especially if they are numerate and like bargaining with publishers; others, especially if their earnings are small, may feel far less happy at the idea of depriving themselves of an agent's skills, but will come to the conclusion that a higher rate of commission will mean that the cost outweighs the benefits. Nevertheless, I would expect the majority of authors to stay with their agents, as seems to be the case in most instances with those agencies which have already put up their fees.

The Agent's Bread and Butter

An agency, especially if is of small or medium size, finds it very difficult to exist without at least one major client, and preferably a handful of big names, 10% of whose earnings will amount to enough to pay a big chunk of the agent's overheads and provide him/her and any other staff in the agency with a living wage. If you have two or three writers on your books who each regularly bring in £100,000 a year, your business obviously has a solid base. But writers in that class are not particularly thick on the ground, and the bigger the agency the greater number of such money-spinners will be needed.

Surely, you may say, the rest of the agent's clients, though each contributes only a comparatively small sum, are the ones who provide the agent's bread-and-butter, while the bestsellers produce the jam. That may apply to large agencies, but for lesser firms one of the headaches is that a major part of the bestseller income has to pay for bread-and-butter rather than jam.

Now, this raises another nasty little thought. It is a fact of life, alas, that the more money people have, in most cases the more they want. George Greenfield, for many years one of Britain's most successful agents, has pointed out that bestselling authors may one day wake up to the fact that they are subsidizing the other writers whom their agent handles. If the income from those top-selling authors were missing, the agent would either find the business totally uneconomic and it would fold, or he/she would have to increase the commission for all the lesser clients. And that might just as easily happen if those bestselling authors, while not wishing to leave the agent, were to decide to demand a cut in the commission taken on their earnings. They could argue, after all, that the agent's work on their behalf, to earn a gross income of £100,000 plus, was no greater than the effort which the same agent would expend to earn £1,000 for a less successful writer. If they were to insist that their agent's commission should be reduced to 5%, Mr Greenfield suggests that the other clients on the list would have to pay 20%. Even if a sliding scale were worked out, so that the agent's percentage was reduced progressively when the author's earnings reached certain levels (for instance: 10% on the first £50,000 earnings, 7½% on the next £50,000 and 5% thereafter), the less successful would still find themselves paying a great deal more commission than they do at present. I suppose we all have to hope that bestselling authors do not wake up to this position, or that, even if they do, they are not tempted to bolster their already large earnings in this way.

Other Charges

As mentioned elsewhere in this book, almost all agents feel it necessary and reasonable to make other charges, and you could expect with most agencies to have to pay for the photocopying of typescripts, for the purchase from the publisher of copies of your book(s), and for foreign postage. These costs are all incurred because the agent is trying to sell various rights for you, and can hardly be regarded as objectionable (but see the comment on this subject in Chapter 8). On the whole, the charges will be modest – although there is no way of economizing on the cost of sending mail abroad, agents have their own photocopying machines and usually want only to meet the actual expense of using them, and the copies of books are bought from the publisher at trade terms.

Some agents claim for other items, such as taxi fares, courier costs, and even 'general expenses', but this hardly seems justifiable unless some agreement on such charges was reached at the time you signed up with the agent. If the agent is involved in spending money exceptionally and at your specific request, or can justify it with some valid explanation, that is of course a different matter.

While the cost to you of having an agent should never take you by surprise, you can't expect to get service for nothing, apart from that initial work mentioned at the beginning of this chapter, so however much of a friend to you your agent is, don't ever allow yourself to forget that he/she is in business to make money – not to exploit you unfairly, but to keep the agency in the black and those who work in it out of personal debt.

Despite this defence of the charges that agents make, I must point out that publishers are not in the habit of recouping their similar costs from their authors, whether the latter have come to them through agents, or direct. And they do not, as a result of one of those strange anomalies in our taxation laws, have to charge VAT on sums paid directly to those authors who are not registered for that tax.

7 The Agent's Contract

The Need for a Formal Agreement

The authors who appointed J.B. Pinker to act for them when he first started his agency were required to sign an agreement with him. Later, when the literary agent had become an established part of the writing and publishing world, the idea of a contract between author and agent lapsed – up to the time of World War II, and even for quite a while after, 'a gentleman's word was his bond' (as they used to say in their politically incorrect way, applying the phrase to both sexes), and that was deemed to be sufficient. Nowadays, as we are all well aware, moral standards have slipped and it's difficult to trust anyone without a written commitment which can be produced, if necessary, in a court of law. But is it really necessary where authors are concerned? If you listen to a group of authors talking you may get the impression that most publishers and some agents are rogues, while all authors are honourable and honest. It just ain't so – as a class, authors are no worse than any other group of people, but they're no better either.

When discussing this subject, one agent recently pointed out that the contract for the publication of a book is between the author and the publisher, not between the agent and the publisher. The agent is merely mentioned in a clause which says that all moneys earned under the contract will be paid to the agent, whose receipt shall be 'a good and valid discharge therefor', and it is the author, not the agent, who signs the contract. The author is therefore at liberty to ask for it to be varied at a later stage if he/she so wishes. And if the author chooses to cut the agent out, the agent has no redress. The agent who was making this point gave the example of an author whom she succeeded in launching after some difficulty, finding a publisher only on the twelfth submission; following the publication of the author's third novel, when he could consider himself to be established, he instructed the publishers to pay all royalties direct to him, saying that he would himself be responsible for paying the agent's commission; the agent has never seen another penny from him.

Authors who were taken on by a literary agency some considerable time ago were probably not asked at the time to sign any form of contract between themselves and the agent, and have continued to work happily with the agent ever since without any formal document. They may have had a letter from the agent setting out the commission terms, but even that matter may have been covered only orally and as and when a particular situation arose. Today, if you find a literary agent who is prepared to take you on, you will almost certainly be asked to sign a contract, or at least to exchange letters setting out the basic terms to which you and the agent will adhere (and such letters are, of course, accepted as legal documents committing both parties to their contents).

To avoid any misunderstanding, it is perhaps worth making clear at this point that agents do not sign contracts with publishers – at least, the overwhelming majority of them do not. Agreements for individual books, as already mentioned, are drawn up between the publisher and the author (or the author's company). And although agents may have their favoured publishing houses to which they prefer to submit any new author's work, they never sign an agreement with the publisher committing them to such a course, or even to an undertaking to submit all of a given author's work to one particular publisher.

The Form of Agreement

The document that an agent asks a new client to countersign as an indication of his/her acceptance may be no more than a fairly brief and informal letter. It might say something like this:

> We charge a commission of x% on all amounts accruing to an author as a result of any agreement which we may make on his/her behalf and with his/her approval, except that on sales in the USA and in translation we charge a commission of y% to include the commission of any sub-agent.
>
> Commission on film and TV sales is by arrangement at the time, but will not normally be less than z%.
>
> We also charge for individual items of postage over £1, and for overseas telephone calls and faxes where necessary.
>
> Unless we specifically agree otherwise we expect to handle your full length work throughout the world in all languages.

The letter may be rather more formal, beginning with such paragraphs as:

> This letter confirms our agreement whereby you appoint us as your agents to act exclusively on your behalf for the sale of all rights in your literary work throughout the world including but not limited to book publishing and volume subsidiary rights, motion picture, television and radio rights.
>
> It is understood that we shall represent your interests to the best of our ability and conduct negotiations on your behalf subject to your approval.
>
> We shall remit to you promptly all money due to you which we receive on your behalf.

And it will almost certainly contain a paragraph to the effect of:

> This agreement may be terminated by either side by sixty days' notice in writing. After termination we shall cease to undertake any negotiation or representation for you, but we shall have the right to continue to receive commission on all contracts which we have negotiated on your behalf, or which derive from them, and on any subsequent extensions or renewals of them. We agree to service all such contracts unless you instruct us otherwise and our commission shall apply to any improved terms on those contracts.

This paragraph sets out one of the arrangements between agents and authors which is regarded as standard practice in the trade. You are free to change agents, or to give up having an agent at all, at any time you like, provided that you give reasonable notice to your existing agent, but if you do cancel your representation the agency has the right to go on taking its commission on the income from any contract which it negotiated for you, including any moneys from sub-licences of that contract. In very exceptional circumstances an agent will give up an ex-client's backlist so that it can be handled by the author's present agent, but this will probably happen only if the backlist is not currently earning and seems unlikely to do so, or if relations between the agent and the ex-client have become so appalling that neither wishes to have anything to do with the other, even at the risk, from the agent's point of view, of losing money.

Such letters as these will probably be sent in duplicate to the author, who will be asked to sign one copy as an indication of acceptance of the terms, and then to return it to the agent.

Some agents use an even more formal document (although still usually in letter form), based on the wording recommended by the Association of Authors' Agents. It may vary slightly from one agency to another, but is likely to be to the following effect:

Dear (Author's name),

1. We are very pleased that you wish us to act us your exclusive worldwide literary agent. We shall represent your interests to the best of our ability, using sub-agents where we consider this appropriate, in relation to the exploitation of all your works but we will not commit you to any agreement without your approval, and you will refer all approaches regarding your work to us. During the term of this Agreement you agree not to employ the services of any other person or company to act for you in the said matters.
2. You are free to enter into this Agreement with us being under no contractual agreement which would in any way conflict with the said Agreement.
3. It is understood that this Agreement shall exclude previously contracted works not negotiated by us. In the event that the

contracts for such works should expire or terminate, you agree that we shall become sole agent for future contracts for such works.

4. We will also do all we can, short of seeking help from lawyers – which will be done only by arrangement with you – to collect money due to you under contracts negotiated through us and we will remit to you promptly money which we collect after deduction only of our commission, any expenses incurred by us on your behalf, and any other money which may be due to us from you.

5. Our commission, to which VAT will be added, will be a percentage of the income arising from all contracts from the exploitation of works you create entered into during the period we represent you at the following rate:

UK sales to publishers, newspapers, magazines, radio and mechanical rights, manufacturers and distributors:	x% of gross proceeds
UK sales to TV, theatre and film:	x% of gross proceeds
US and foreign languages sales throughout the world to outlets as above:	y% of gross proceeds

No commission shall be deducted on prize moneys, grants or PLR earnings.

If you are registered for VAT you may reclaim that VAT paid on the commission. Should you receive any income direct we shall be entitled to receive from you our commission plus VAT.

6. You, in turn, undertake with us that all contracts relating to the exploitation of your works entered into whilst we are your agent will include a provision whereby the income payable under them is to be paid to us, both during and after our agency period. You authorize us to make the deductions from the income referred to above. It is also agreed that we are entitled to be joined as a party to every contract for exploitation to enable us to receive and collect such income.

7. Normal expenses in connection with offering the works and dealing with contracts and income arising therefrom shall not be charged to you. However, extraordinary expenses shall be charged to you but these will be deducted wherever possible when payments are received for your works. These extraordinary expenses include photocopying, proof copies, books bought by the agent for promotional purposes or for submission to publishers abroad, messenger and courier services, legal expenses, faxes and other exceptional expenses which may be

incurred but only with your prior approval or which if we are unable to contact you may be reasonably incurred in the absence of such approval. In the event of termination of this Agreement a bill for any outstanding expenses will be submitted and details of outstanding negotiations referred to in Clause 8 shall not notwithstanding the fourteen day period referred to be disclosed until payment of such a bill has been made.

8. Our agency will continue until terminated by either party on giving not less than fourteen days written notice to the other whereupon, unless we both agree otherwise, we shall cease to represent you but we shall continue to be entitled to commission in respect of all income arising from contracts for the exploitation of your works entered into while we represented you and from all extensions and renewals of such contracts. We shall also be entitled to commission where the income arises from a contract following on a submission we made to a publisher before we ceased to represent you where that contract was signed after we ceased to represent you.

9. While we shall take all reasonable care of the manuscripts, outlines, illustrative materials, books and other property which you may entrust to us we will not be liable in respect of their loss or damage.

10. You shall have the right to assign all or part of the works to any other party and will notify us at least ten days in advance of any such assignment. Such assignees shall at the same time confirm to us in writing their agreement to assume all your obligations in connection with this Agreement in respect to such works.

11. This Agreement sets out our entire understanding and shall bind our heirs executors administrators and assigns.

An agreement such as this will probably also have attached an Appendix detailing, formally, the meanings of such words as 'works', 'exploitation', etc.

The author/agent contract quoted above may seem a formidable document indeed, and one which is designed almost exclusively to protect the agent rather than the client. In fact, it is not unfair in any major respect, but, according to circumstances, you as the author, might wish to restrict its scope by excluding various kinds of writing (so that the agent is not to act for you, for instance in respect of any journalism that you may undertake), and to make certain other minor alterations, such as a rewording of Clause 7 to make it clear that not only none of the 'exceptional' expenses, but also none of those described as 'extraordinary' would be charged to you without your consent. However frightening the agreement may be, it does not really say anything which is outside the normal understanding which exists between an author and an agent – and this includes not seeking legal advice, which could be expensive to the author, without his/her prior consent – and it should not be regarded as in any way damaging to the friendship which should be an essential part of the relationship.

I understand that the Association of Authors' Agents may soon recommend that agreements between agents and authors should contain a clause emphasizing the author's responsibility to read and approve any agreements sent to them for signature by the agent. This is designed to prevent any author from complaining at some point of difficulty that he/she did not realize that such and such a provision was included in the contract – 'I thought it would be Ok because my agent had vetted it, so I signed without reading it.'

The Agent's Commitment and Responsibilities

The Association of Authors' Agents has not only prepared a recommended agreement to set out the terms of business between agent and client, but has also drawn up a Code of Practice for its members, and although some of its provisions refer to the way agencies regard and deal with each other, it is designed above all for the protection of the author.

The Code of Practice of the Association of Authors' Agents

a) No member shall knowingly represent an author who is the client of another agency, without the agreement of such agency, whether or not that agency is a member of the Association. Failure to enquire as to an author's agency relationship shall be considered negligence and a violation of this rule.

b) No member of the Association shall charge a reading fee on his/her own behalf to an author except in circumstances approved by a majority of the Committee.

c) All members shall account faithfully to their authors, paying within not more than 21 days of the money being cleared in the member's bank account, for all sums due to their authors unless instructed otherwise by their authors or unless such sums total less than £25.

d) Members shall furnish promptly to their authors any information and material which the author may reasonably request in connection with his/her business.

e) No member shall act for an author after his/her authority to do so, whether oral or written, has terminated, except that

- i) the member shall not be debarred from continuing to act if so instructed in writing by the author and
- ii) the member shall continue to take commission in respect of agreements entered into previously with third parties by the member on the author's behalf and appropriate commission in respect of negotiations carried out on the author's behalf which are subsequently concluded by the author or a new agent.

f) No member shall charge a fee to the author beyond his/her regular commission as notified to the Association without the author's prior consent in writing.

A member may not, without informing his/her author in writing in advance, represent in any transaction both his/her author as a vendor of services or copyright material and any other interest as purchaser of such material and must declare to the author in writing any proprietary or profitable interest in any contract apart from that of normal agency commission. A member may in exceptional circumstances make special commission arrangements with an author provided that he/she obtains the author's prior consent in writing. Members are strongly advised to consult the Committee if they are in any doubt whatsoever as to the propriety of such special arrangement. The Committee shall have power to decide on the acceptability to the Association of any such special arrangement which comes to its notice and to require the member in question to amend to its satisfaction any such arrangements which in its unanimous view it deems unacceptable.

g) A member shall not use or communicate to others information relating to an author's affairs confidentially given to him/her except as required by law.

h) A member shall allow his/her authors at all reasonable times the right to verify and authenticate any statement of account concerning that author and shall submit promptly and regularly to the author full details of any transaction handled by the member.

i) All members shall establish a bank account for their clients' money separately from the member's general business and personal accounts except in circumstances notified to and approved by a majority of the Committee.

All complaints made against members for alleged violation of any provision of the code of practice shall be considered by the full Committee of the Association who shall have the right to expel any member against whom a significant and material breach of the code of practice is upheld. Such a decision shall be taken unanimously by the Committee. Any member against whom a complaint has been lodged shall have the right to appear in person before the Committee to hear and answer such complaint. In the event of a dispute between member agencies over a matter of professional practice, other than an alleged violation of any provisions of the code of practice, the Committee may, if requested by the parties, act as arbitrators.

The problem with the Code of Practice is that the Association of Authors' Agents has no real sanction to employ against any member who offends unforgivably, other than expulsion from the Association, which might not particularly worry the punished agency. Nevertheless, the Code's heart is in the right place (if a Code may be said to have a heart), and it seems to work.

8 The Published Author's View of Agents

The Society of Authors Survey

As has already been mentioned, the Society of Authors was cautious, rather than entirely enthusiastic, in its attitude to literary agents in the early days of their existence. Currently, the Society works happily with most agents when the occasion arises, and frequently joins with them when they have common cause.

However, the relationship between an author and an agent tends to be so personal that it is not altogether easy for an organization to be aware of exactly how its members are getting on with a different group of people, and in late 1993 the Society conducted a survey of its members, asking them to fill in a long and detailed questionnaire about their literary agents. The results of the survey were published in the Society's journal, the *Author*, in the Spring of 1994.

The Society of Authors has some 5,000 members. Of these, approximately half, including almost all those who work in academic and educational fields, do not have agents; of the remaining 2,500 members, just under 500 replied. Not a large number, you might think, too small, in fact, to be worth considering – although most organizations sending out a similar mailing shot would be delighted with a 20% return. However, the answers seemed to be genuinely representative, and in general terms showed a remarkable unanimity.

The responses covered 106 agencies. Several of the larger agencies received more than twenty-five reports each, which means, of course, that many others were referred to by one author only. In assessing the capabilities of the different agencies one has to be very cautious in making judgments about those about which few reports were received.

Authors Love Their Agents

The main fact which emerged was that an overwhelming majority of authors love their agents. The key question was 'Are you generally satisfied with the service provided?' Authors are often revealed in the pages of *The Author* to be a somewhat disgruntled group of people, with a tendency to feel hard done by and to see themselves as the Cinderellas of the book world, with publishers cast permanently as the Ugly Sisters (understudied by reviewers and sometimes by booksellers). If anyone can play the part of the Fairy Godmother, it has to be the agent. No fewer than 73% of the authors replying to the survey replied that they were indeed satisfied with the service they got, and a very high proportion of those added words like 'very', 'absolutely' or 'delighted'. A further 10% replied favourably, but with some (usually slight) reservations. 13% partly balanced this general contentment with a firm denial of any satisfaction whatsoever, and the remaining 4% were not completely disenchanted with their agents, but felt some doubts about them. So there were 17% negative results to be set against 83% in favour of agents, with almost all of the positives being generous in their praise.

The Author's Requirements

The authors were asked what they wanted from their agents. Top of the list, to no one's surprise, was the placing of the author's work with a publisher, including foreign and subsidiary rights, the negotiation of contracts, and the collecting and checking of moneys due. The next most important points were the friendship, the support and the encouragement that an agent can give, and also editorial advice at typescript stage, career guidance, and the provision of ideas. Naturally, the authors did not all have the same requirements and reactions, so there were many other aspects of the agent's work which were singled out for praise, including acting as a buffer between authors and publishers in negotiations and disputes, the agent's experience and knowledge of the market, good communications, and the fact that the agent is on the author's side.

And did they get all that they wanted? What did the authors think were the most important strengths of their agents? Friendship, loyalty and encouragement were mentioned even more often than negotiating skills. Approval was given to many other factors – personal attention, the agent's availability (much more reliable than that of a publisher, partly because agents, as has already been mentioned, don't seem to spend half their time in meetings), the high reputation of the agency (which may enhance that of the author), knowledge of the market, honesty, efficiency and attention to detail, and the first-rate quality of the advice which could be obtained from the agent, whether it was in detailed editorial criticisms or in more general matters. And several authors said that their agent 'understands my work' (implying strongly, of course, that certain other people don't).

The Size of the Agency

Comments were frequently made about the size of the agency. Some authors were clearly happy to be with one of the larger concerns, which was able to deal with all aspects of the author's work under the one roof, with different members of the staff looking after their own specialities. Other were equally pleased to be with a small, one-person business, not so much because of being a large fish in a small pond (some would have been fairly small fishes in a pond of any size), but because they felt that they were getting close personal attention all the time from someone who knew and worked on every aspect of their work.

Loyalty

One of the most interesting points to emerge was that authors tended to stay with the agent with whom they had first started. 55% of those responding had had only one agent, 31% had had two (but a large proportion of these had changed only because the first agent had died or gone out of business), and the remaining 14% had had more than two. With those figures it is not surprising that one of the other virtues that authors saw in their agents was that of stability – there is usually continuity in the author-agent relationship, in contrast with the changing modern world of publishing, in which editors move from firm to firm, and companies amalgamate and are taken over and go out of business with far more frequency than in the past.

Contracts

In response to a question about whether the author had a contract with the agent, 30% said that they had. This may seem a low figure, but the idea of a formal contract with an agency has been revived only comparatively recently, and many of those replying to the survey began their relationship with their agents long before it again became at all common to have a formal arrangement. Moreover, there may have been some confusion since many agencies use an exchange of correspondence rather than a formal contract, and although the letters are in fact a legally acceptable agreement, some of the authors may not have considered them as such. None of those who said they had a contract seemed to find it in any way a burden or unreasonable, but one author did point out that a certain large agency had begun to use wording saying that it is 'hereby irrevocably authorized to act as agents for the author'. No author should accept such a clause – the author should always be free to leave the agent at will and for any reason at all (subject, of course, to the standard practices after leaving, as explained in Chapter 7).

The Negative Side

Those who responded to the survey were asked to express any dissatisfactions, even if their overall feeling was that agents were absolute darlings and of immense value to the author. Four subjects came up fairly often. The first of these was the charges made by the agent in addition to the normal percentages on the author's earnings. Very few cases were mentioned of reading fees, and these appeared to concern only first-time authors. But the majority of agents pass on the costs of photocopying and of the purchase of additional copies of a published book in order to submit it to foreign publishers, and postage to destinations abroad is also sometimes debited on the author's account. Some of the respondents in the survey felt that these were ordinary business expenses which should be borne by the agent, and an even larger number, while prepared to pay the charges without protest to the agent, quite clearly resented what appeared to them as meanness (it may, of course, seem cheese-paring in an individual case, but you can perhaps see the agent's point of view when you think how these costs must mount up over a period of time for all the clients on his/her list).

The second aspect which produced some rather negative replies related to the agent's efforts in selling United States, translation, film, radio and television rights. Quite a lot of authors felt that their agents could have done better in these directions. They may be right – not all agents are absolute whizzes when they are away from their familiar stamping-ground of British book publishers. On the other hand, if any agents had been asked to comment, they might have said that authors nearly always have unrealistic expectations of what foreign and specialist sales their books are capable of achieving, and lack of success doesn't always mean lack of effort.

The third critical point which was raised was that some agents seemed interested only in the big name authors on their lists and paid little attention to the smaller fry. It should be made clear that most of those who made this criticism were still happy with their agents' performance in general, and were obviously sensible enough to understand that no one can expect equal treatment in this unequal world. If you have any difficulty in coming to terms with the idea that agents may dance attendance more enthusiastically on some authors than on others, have another look at the discussion of agents' commission in Chapter 6.

The last of the major adverse comments concerned the agent's insistence on taking commission on a deal which the author has initiated and negotiated directly with a publisher or other purchaser. 'The agent has done nothing – why should he/she get paid?' The agent's reply is that his/her other services will be required to monitor everything else connected with the sale, and if you want to do deals on your own, it is always possible to sever your connection with the agency, provided that you do it in advance of whatever negotiation you have in mind and that the work concerned is a new one with which the agent has not been concerned. Apart from any arrangement which may be made at the beginning of the relationship that the agency will handle only an author's fiction, perhaps, or everything other than journalism and radio and television appearances, agents always expect to take their cut on all deals which are made, whatever the circumstances.

Naturally, there were other niggles – 'my agent sulks if I don't take up his suggestions', 'unbusinesslike, inefficient', 'he can't spot a good writer if one jumps up and bites him', 'my agent is too aggressive' and, in contradiction, 'my agent isn't aggressive enough'. There were occasional stories to make one's hair stand on end, such as the agent who suggested that one of her well-known clients should take a consultancy course with her (the agent) in order to 'reorientate the author's strategy' at a cost of 30 guineas for each of the six sessions (and since no one has talked of guineas for years, you can work out that the sum would be astonishingly greater in today's terms), or the agent who suggested that a client should turn over all his material on a proposed non-fiction book to another author on the agent's list, because the agent would then be able to get a much larger advance for it.

If you are still hoping to find an agent who will take you on, don't be put off by these stories. You might be very unlucky and land up with one of the very few unreliable, inefficient, unbusinesslike and generally useless agents – as has already been said, in any group of people and in any spheres of business there are always bound to be the odd ones who behave badly. The majority of agents can be relied upon to give you the kind of service which will add you to the 83% of satisfied customers revealed by the survey.

9 The Publisher's View of Agents

Early Reactions

As has already been mentioned, publishers were not enraptured when the first literary agents appeared on the scene. William Heinemann, who regarded agents as parasites, is credited by some with the saying, 'The agent is to the publisher as the knife is to the throat' (although others attribute the dictum to an unknown American publisher). The antipathy persisted long after Heinemann's death in 1918. As late as the 1960's Stanley Unwin was content to leave a whole series of disparaging remarks about agents in what was then the latest edition of his classic book *The Truth About Publishing*, and one of his contemporaries, Walter Harrap, used always to refer to the literary agents Pearn, Pollinger & Higham as 'Pig, Pig and Pig', not so much because he wanted to insult Nancy Pearn, Laurence Pollinger and David Higham personally, but because in those words he expressed his hatred of all agents.

The Present Day

Do publishers think the same way about agents nowadays? There is perhaps a certain ambivalence in their attitude, but, as I have already said, agents are powerful people in the literary world, and most (but not all) publishers do their best to curry favour with them.

To find out more I asked a representative group of publishers, including both large and small concerns, and both independents and some members of conglomerates, to answer a number of questions for me. I am grateful to them for responding so readily.

The first question was: *Do you like working with agents, or do you prefer not to?* The majority of replies expressed no great feeling either way, suggesting that the publishers concerned were equally happy to work through agents or with authors direct. One firm, Severn House, expressed a strong preference for agented books, mainly because books which have been accepted by an agent can be guaranteed to have some degree of quality, and would not have been sent to Severn House if they were not suitable to their list, and additionally, since Severn House specializes in the hardcover library market and publishes mostly established authors, the majority of whom already have agents. Their liking for agented books is not surprising since the paragraph which the company supplies for *Writers' and Artists' Yearbook* and *The Writer's Handbook* states unequivocally that it is interested in submissions only from agents. In contrast, one of the independent publishers does not like working with agents, prefers not to, and in response to the question said so quite firmly, ending by quoting from *Much Ado About Nothing*: 'Let every eye negotiate for itself and trust no agent.' Clearly, however, this publisher is in a minority.

I then asked: *Do you think that in general agents are a Good Thing, or a Necessary Evil?* On the whole, the publishers seemed to be of the opinion that agents were OK, and even the anti-agent publisher cited in the last paragraph said that they were a Good Thing 'for some authors'. Patrick Janson-Smith of Transworld Publishers said: 'By and large I think agents are a Good Thing. Then again, in my darker moments, I think they're a Necessary Evil or, worse, an Unnecessary Evil! No question: there are quite a number of totally useless agents around – those who grab the money and then disappear from view until it's time for the next tranche of money to be handed over. A good agent is one who takes an interest beyond that (without being overbearing in his interest).' In similar vein, Christopher Sinclair-Stevenson, Managing Director of Sinclair-Stevenson (now part of the Reed Group) said: 'Some agents are worth 1% commission, others are worth their weight in gold. Most authors need them, a few don't. From a publisher's point of view, they are occasionally a necessary evil, more often an essential good.'

The third question was: *Are there some agents you like to work with and others who are a pain?* This question might have been considered rather a waste of time, since it elicited from most of my correspondents the predictable answer that they had no problems in working with some agents, but found others less pleasant to deal with. However, two answers seem to me well worth quoting here. Karin Stoecker of Harlequin Mills & Boon made the cogent comment: 'Agents are a pain when they don't understand the publishing business, when they create unrealistic expectations for the author, intimidate the author or otherwise behave in an unprofessional or unethical manner including putting their own agenda first (quick sale vs author career objectives), misrepresenting author to publisher or vice versa, withholding information, delaying payments, or when they don't honour the terms of the current contract. Merely annoying are those agents who neglect to know the publisher's market and requirements, who focus on unimportant or non-negotiable matters, and who never return phone calls or follow up in timely fashion.' And Diane Pearson of Transworld Publishers produced a splendid tirade about bad agents: 'There are good ones and bad ones – the good ones I like working with, the bad ones often serve to mess up a deal and make mischief. What makes me angrier than anything is when one has found an author oneself, got her nicely launched, sold sub rights in many areas and generally done a super job, to have an agent home in, convince the author she needs an agent, try to raise the advance to an unrealistic level, and just plug in to all the foreign publishers and TV directors which we have established the author with. My advice to authors who have no agent but do have a publisher is to check out that publisher's foreign rights department. We have an excellent one. They can easily provide, and do, everything an agent can.' Ms Pearson continued: 'My main beef about bad agents is that they so rarely go out and find new authors, work with them to get the best book possible, then place them thoughtfully and well with the right editor/house. In my experience (and we have quite a few authors whom we have taken from scratch, worked with, etc, etc), agents scan publishers' lists in order to find unagented authors ... The bad agents are not interested in the book except as revenue for themselves.' Before all authors reading this decide that Ms Pearson has a down on the whole tribe of agents, let me say that she then goes on to praise highly certain of them who meet her criteria, among which are their habits of working with their authors, only submitting work when they think it ready, being concerned about the development of the author's career, and being realistic about advances, not just going for the highest figure and leaving the author with an unearned advance and a general bad feeling at the publisher. I suspect that most sensible publishers would agree with those criteria.

Paul Scherer of Transworld Publishers made the further point that too many agents know very little about the publishing process or about how quickly things change within it. This is partly because many of them have never worked in publishing and partly because inevitably their main points of contact are with editors who, in many – especially the largest – companies, do not have close involvement with all aspects of the business. The author who wants to understand the publishing process would do well to pick a publishing house with a known reputation for real author involvement in all aspects of the business. It is really only by direct contact like this, rather than dealing with the publisher entirely through the literary agent, that the author can understand something of the whys and wherefores of what is happening to his or her book. Literary agents, equally, have the duty to know a wide variety of people in publishing (not just editors) and make real efforts to understand how the publishing process works. And that again can only be done by frequent and widespread contact and homework.

An inquiry as to whether there were any major agents which the publisher did not deal with, and whether this was at the agent's choice or the publisher's, produced answers which seem to indicate that, if the authors and books are ones they want, the majority will deal with any agent, whether they like him/her or not.

Next I asked: *When you dream up an idea for a book, do you normally go to an agent, or find an author for it in some other way?* The majority of the editors who replied seem most often to be able to think of a specific author for any book which they originate in this way, so the involvement of an agent depends on whether the author they have in mind is agented or not. This means that they would rarely simply take an idea to an agent in the hope that he/she would be able to supply a suitable author who was previously unknown to the publisher.

Do you ever suggest to an author who has come to you direct that he/she should go to an agent? All my publishers replied in the affirmative. Erica Hunningher of Frances Lincoln Ltd said: 'It's good to free the author/publisher relationship of the financial aspects.' But she went on: 'If I know the terms I'm proposing are virtually non-negotiable (i.e. 'take it or leave it'!), I'd discourage the author from engaging an agent.' Christopher Sinclair-Stevenson made the point: 'It depends on the film and television rights potential. I believe that a good publisher ought to be able to handle most rights as well as an agent, but the film and TV world is too complex and fluid for anyone but a specialist.' None of my respondents mentioned, as I hoped they might, the possibility of persuading an author to go to an agent if that author is clearly going to be extremely difficult, questioning everything, arguing over every detail, and living in a permanent state of discontent. There are authors like that, and publishers do sometimes try to protect themselves by interposing an agent.

The next question, which produced very interesting answers, was: *Can you give any indication, however rough, of what proportion of the books you publish are agented?* The figures given varied widely, but the two publishers who take only 10% (Souvenir Press) and 15% (A & C Black) of their books from agents are out of line with the rest, whose percentages went from 50% (Frances Lincoln), to 60% (Hale), 80% (Headline, Sinclair-Stevenson), 90% (Transworld), and 95% (HarperCollins,

Severn House). Although this would seem to indicate that would-be authors are right to believe that you really should get an agent if you want to break into print, the figures are distorted to some extent by the fact that a substantial part of any publisher's output consists of books by authors whom that firm has published before, and often regularly, and most such authors have agents, although they may not have done when they first started. But publishers are always looking for new authors, and although they may take more beginner writers from agents rather than direct, this is because, as has already been explained, the books which are submitted to them by agents have already been through the agent's sieve; the dross has been eliminated, and the quality of the wares which the agent is peddling therefore tends to be higher than that of the slushpile. Nevertheless, publishers do trawl through the slushpile with care, and will happily take on an unagented book which they find in it, provided that it reaches a high enough standard and is suited to their list.

My penultimate question was: *When you take on an agented book, do you more often accept the agent's form of contract or insist on your own, or does this depend on which agent it is?* The answers suggest that while the majority of publishers like to use their own contracts, and will insist on doing so whenever they can, most of them will accept the agent's version if they have no alternative. But in any case, almost all of them appear to have worked out what are rather oddly referred to as 'boilerplate' (i.e. standard) contracts with most agents, so although there may be considerable negotiation over individual terms, the basic wording has been accepted by both sides.

Finally, I asked for any comments. Not surprisingly, some of my respondents, having already answered my questions at some length, felt that further words were unnecessary. But I was struck by what two of the publishers said. Karin Stoecker of Harlequin Mills & Boon gave some good advice, neatly expressed: 'Selecting an agent is much like buying a pair of shoes; they should be a good, comfortable fit; right for the occasion – not merely in fashion at the moment.' One of the other publishers underlined a couple of my own points in the following words: 'I have always thought that the great benefit of agents both to authors and to publishers is that they should make authors fully au fait with the book world. It is all very well a publisher trying to explain to an author why his first hardcover novel is not going to be widely displayed at Heathrow, but only an agent can give the kind of objective advice which an author will accept. Secondly, I have a gripe about some agents who very understandably make it a policy to work with a small number of publishers or offer a book only to four or five publishers, still nevertheless give the authors the impression that the book has been offered to everyone. One so often sees reports by authors of their books having been turned down by every publisher and then becoming a bestseller. It is abundantly clear to me that very few books indeed make the full round of publishers, particularly the right ones.'

Summing Up

What can be learnt from this report on my mini-survey by the author who wants to get into print and is wondering whether to try to get an agent before approaching a publisher? I think the answer is that the replies prove that it is indeed good to have an agent, even if it's not essential. But it is also clear that it is vital to get one of the good ones. To make sure that you don't fall into the hands of one of the other kind, it is advisable to do some market research. Find out what other people think of any agent you have in mind (this probably depends on whether you know any published authors whom you can quiz on the subject), or ask the Society of Authors or the Writers' Guild (which depends on your being a member), or ask your publisher (which depends on already having one). If you have no way of checking up, then you must simply take pot luck. However, you can still make certain in a personal interview, before you commit yourself, that you and your proposed agent will be compatible, and that he/she seems to have his/her feet on the ground and shows no signs of being economical with the truth.

Remember, if it doesn't work out, there is no reason why you shouldn't leave the agent and seek a new one, or work on your own. There is equally no reason why you should not be at the beginning of a long and fruitful relationship, which you will not wish to abandon, with one of Christopher Sinclair-Stevenson's 'other' agents, who are worth their weight in gold.

Index

AAA, *see* Association of Authors' Agents
academic writers, 14, 18, 23, 105
acceptance, clause, 55
advance, 21, 51–2, 53, 55, 66, 87, 115
agency, size of, 24, 85, 107
agent
  as intermediary in disputes, 62–6
  author's approach to, 27–31
  author's change of, 40–1, 97–8
  author's choice of, 23–6
  author's loyalty to, 24–5, 108
  author's need for, 17–21
  author's relationship with, 19, 32–4, 40, 65–6, 75–9, 82–3, 95–101, 106–11
agent's
  actions after author's death, 72–3
  advice on author's career, 19, 23, 38, 75–9, 107
  advice on author's financial matters, 69–71
  approach to publishers, 44–50, 106
  availability, 81–2, 107
  charges, 87–93, 109
  code of practice, 15, 69, 101–3
  commission, 19, 32, 37–8, 88–92, 110
  contract negotiation, 19, 51–9, 106
  contracts with authors, 39, 95–101, 108
  dealing with author's moneys, 66–71, 101–2, 106, 107
  editorial advice, 23, 38, 39, 43–4, 65, 76, 107
  encouragement of author, 78, 80, 107
  expenses, 37–8, 90–3
  experience, 35–6, 38, 57–8, 64, 71, 72, 78, 107
  knowledge of market, 35–6, 38, 57–8, 107, 116
  legal expertise, 72
  loyalty to author, 107
  promotion of author, 58, 79–80
  reading fees, 87
  relationship with authors, 80, 107
  relationship with publishers, 35–6, 44–50, 61–6, 83
  selection of clients, 34–5
  sub-agents, 57, 58, 88
agreement forms, 53–4, 55–6, 118
agreements, publishers', *see* contracts, publishers'
Aitken, Stone & Wylie, 13
anthology rights, 56
articles, 17, 89
Association of Authors' Agents, 14–15, 25, 40, 69, 87, 98, 101–3
  Code of Practice, 15, 69, 101–3
auctions, 47–9
Author, the, 105, 106
Author's Empty Purse & the Rise of the Literary Agent, The, 9
Authors' Foundation, The, 70
Author's Guide to Publishing, An, 23, 55

author's
approach to an agent, 27–31
change of publisher, 76–8
choice of agent, 23–6
loyalty to an agent, 108
need for an agent, 17–21
problems with a publisher, 62–5
relationship with an agent, 19, 32–4, 40, 65–6, 75–9, 82–3

Ballantyne, John and James, 9
bestsellers, 8, 19, 24, 37, 73, 91–2
Black, A & C, 117
Blond, Anthony, 7, 86
blurb, 55, 62, 71
Bolt, David, 20
Book Book, The, 86
bookclub rights, 22, 56, 58, 72
Burghes, A.M., 10

career advice, 19, 23, 38, 75–9, 107
Colles, W.M., 10
commission, agent's, 19, 32, 37–8, 88–92, 110
commissions, agent's procurement of, 73–5
consultation, 55
contract negotiation, 19, 51–9
contracts
agents', 39, 95–101, 108
publishers', 53–9, 95–103, *passim*
copy-editing, 62–3
Curtis Brown, 11, 13
Curtis Brown Group, 11, 15, 24, 25

dramatic rights, 18, 58, 89

editorial advice, 23, 38, 39, 43–4, 65, 76, 107
educational writers, 14, 18, 23, 105
electronic rights, 56, 59

Farquharson, John, 11, 13
film rights, 18, 24, 33, 56–8, 89, 109, 117
foreign rights, 33, 56, 57, 58, 80, 88, 106, 109
Forster, John, 9

Gabriel, Jüri, 69
Good Companions, The, 19
Gordon, Giles, 37
grant of rights, 56–9
grants, 70, 99
Greenfield, George, 91, 92

Hadfield, John, 19
Hale, Robert, 117
Harlequin Mills & Boon, 115, 118
HarperCollins, 117
Harrap, Walter, 113
Heath, A.M., 13
Heinemann, William, 12, 113
Hepburn, James, 9
Higham, David, 13, 113
Hodder Headline, 117
Hughes Massie, 13
Hunningher, Erica, 117

jackets, 55, 62
Janson-Smith, Patrick, 114
journalism, 22, 100, 110

large print rights, 56
Lewes, G.H., 9
Lincoln, Frances, 117

magazines, 17, 28, 89
Minimum Terms Agreement, 14, 54–6, 61, 66
Mitchell, Charles, 9

Nash, J. Eveleigh, 10
negotiation of agreements, 19, 51–9
newspapers, 17, 28, 89

option, 55–6

paperback rights, 56, 58, 72
Pearn, Pollinger & Higham, 13, 113
Pearn, Nancy, 13, 113
Pearson, Diane, 115–16
Peters, A.D., 13, 19, 38
Pinker, J.B., 11, 95
poetry, 17
Pollinger, Gerald, 13
Pollinger, Laurence, 13, 113

Pollinger, Murray, 13
Priestley, J.B., 19
print quantity, 62
prize moneys, 99
Public Lending Right, 79, 99
publication date, 55, 62
publicity, 48–9, 55, 62, 63
publishers' agreements, 53–9
Publishing Game, The, 7
publishing problems, 62–5

radio rights, 18, 109, 110
Rayner Claire, 74
reading fees, 87, 101
Regional Arts Associations, 70
remainders, 55
reversion of rights, 71–2
Royal Literary Fund, The, 70
royalties, 7, 21, 51–2, 54–5, 66–9, 84, 87, 90
royalty statements, 19, 58, 66–9, 85

Scherer, Paul, 116
serial rights, 56, 57, 58, 89
Severn House, 114, 118
Shaw, Bernard, 12
short stories, 17, 22, 89
Sinclair-Stevenson, Christopher, 114–15, 120
slushpile, 19–20
Society of Authors, The, 10, 12, 14, 22–3, 54–5, 59, 105, 119
Society of Authors survey of agents, 105–11
Souvenir Press, 117
Stoecker, Karin, 115, 118
sub-licenses, 20, 56, 59, 71, 98
subsidiary rights, 18, 52, 55, 56, 58, 59, 67, 106, 109

television rights, 18, 24, 33, 58, 89, 109, 110, 117
translation rights, 33, 56, 57, 58, 80, 88, 106, 109
Transworld Publishers, 114, 115, 116, 117
Truth About Publishing, The, 12, 113

Understanding Publishers' Contracts, 55, 56
Unwin, Stanley, 12, 113
US rights, 20, 33, 56, 57, 58, 88, 106, 109

VAT, 69–70, 89–90, 93, 99
volume rights, 22, 56

Watt, A.P., 9–10, 11–12, 88
Watts, Dunton, T., 9
Wells, H.G., 12
Winant, Ursula, 74
world rights, 56
Writers' & Artists' Yearbook, 14, 15, 22, 23, 25, 26, 114
Writer's Guild of Great Britain, The, 14, 23, 54–5, 59, 119
Writer's Handbook, The, 15, 22, 23, 25, 26, 114